EARLY LITERACY
IN THE CLASSROOM

A New Standard for Young Readers

Helen Depree and Sandra Iversen

Contents

1 Introduction   5

2 A Balanced Language Program   7
Controlling the Reading and Writing Processes   8
Reading for Enjoyment and Experience   9
Personal Writing   9
Reading for Information   9
Writing for a Variety of Purposes   9
Functional Reading   9
Writing to Extend and Clarify Thought   10

3 Organisation and Management   11
How Do We Do This?   11
Suggestions for the First Week   14
The Second Week and Beyond   16
Looking for Emergent Readers   17
Looking for Early and Fluency Level Readers   18

4 Strategic Reading   19
What is a Strategic Reader?   19
Interactions and Dialogue   22
Texts that Help Emergent, Early, and Fluency Reading   24

5 Scaffolded Instruction   25
Scaffolding in the Major Approaches   25

6 Reading Approaches   31
Reading to Children   31
Language Experience   32
Shared Reading   34
Guided Reading   39
Independent Reading   43
Using a Single Book in Different Ways   44

7 Responses to Texts   47
Activities   47
Responses to Literature   48

8 Monitoring and Evaluating Children's Reading   55
Making Progress   55
The Record of Reading Behaviour   55

9 Writing   65
Writing Purposes and Forms   73
Monitoring Children's Writing   77
Analysing Writing Samples   78
Reluctant Writers   80

10 Oral Language   87
    Communication   87
    Ideas to Assist Oral Language Development   88
    Oral Language as an Aid to Literacy   89
    Monitoring Oral Language Development   90

11 Factual Texts   91
    Accessing, Organising, and Presenting Information   91
    Types of Factual Text   92

12 Technology and Literacy   93
    Learning Experiences and Outcomes   100

13 Drama as a Medium for Learning   103
    Steps for Using Drama   103

Glossary   105

References   109

Appendix   111

1 Introduction

Children bring many varied language experiences and social and cultural values with them to school. In the preschool environment, children build theories that they refine and adapt as they notice new things in their environment. By refining and adapting these theories, children raise their levels of understanding. It is the same for reading, writing, and speaking. Those children who have engaged in many conversations, who have been read to, and who have had the opportunity to experiment with pencil and paper already have a strongly developed aptitude for literacy learning when they arrive at school. A stimulating language program and a sensitive, interested, and caring teacher will allow learning to proceed according to each child's needs. In such a classroom, children develop an enthusiastic attitude towards learning. They are invited to ask questions of each other, as well as of you, and also to explore the classroom environment to find out about things for themselves. With guidance, children soon become competent communicators and independent readers and writers.

Early Literacy in the Classroom is designed to help you, the teacher, maximise your children's learning during the first three years of school. It sets language learning in the context of a balanced literacy program that includes oral, written, and visual modes of language. We have placed the emphasis in this book on the learning of reading and writing. This is not to suggest that the other language areas of listening and speaking, and viewing and presenting information are not important. Our emphasis is simply because we all know that if children do not learn to read and write in the first three years at school, it is very difficult for them to catch up with their peers at a later date. Feelings of failure and frustration can then lead to other learning and behavioural problems.

Our philosophies of reading and writing are simple. We believe that children need to be able to:

- comprehend and decode in reading;
- formulate ideas and spell in writing.

We believe that there are certain skills and strategies pertinent to the acquisition of both reading and writing processes that children must acquire to become independent readers and writers. We do not believe that these skills and strategies are best learned from a "top-down" approach that focuses heavily on reading for meaning with little attention to print, or writing without attention to spelling. We also do not believe that these skills and strategies are best learned from a "bottom-up" approach that would not involve reading text or composing stories until certain items of knowledge and phonic rules had been mastered. Rather, we suggest that children use a *range* of strategies depending on the complexity of the text, sometimes functioning at the level of meaning and sometimes functioning at the word, syllable, or letter level.

We contend that reading and writing are problem-solving activities and that beginning readers and writers need to know how to use their initiative, building on what they know about the world and how language works to make connections and to generate new learning. They need freedom, time, and encouragement to test out ideas and solutions, inquire and research, and to evaluate their current learning. They also need explicit instruction. The provision of all these components is essential.

Chapter 2, "A Balanced Language Program", describes classroom programs that provide a context in which early literacy learning can take place. Chapter 4, "Strategic Reading", sets out in more detail the strategies that emerge as children take control over increasingly difficult texts. Chapters 9 and 10 explore important aspects of writing and oral language.

In order to become competent and independent in literacy tasks as soon as possible, children need you to:

- read and reflect on current research;
- understand the skills and strategies that children need to control;
- respond to children's particular needs;
- design appropriate programs.

These programs should be based on children's prior social, cultural and language knowledge, their differing learning styles and their developing literacy competencies, rather than trying to make all children fit into prepackaged, lock step programs.

Successful teachers need to be managers, evaluators, facilitators, and models. As managers, you need to be able to manage the children, the resources, the program, and the learning environment. Chapter 3, "Organisation and Management", gives detailed suggestions for setting up a literacy program at the beginning of the year. Chapter 7, "Responses to Text", presents ways in which children can be encouraged to work independently by responding to texts in different ways. Sections of Chapter 6, "Reading Approaches", and Chapter 9, "Writing", also provide valuable information on management.

The importance of the dialogue between you and the children cannot be over-emphasised. It is during these interactions that you are able to facilitate learning powerfully and effectively. Chapters 5 and 6, "Scaffolded Instruction" and "Reading Approaches", show how as a facilitator and model you can assist children's literacy learning.

Ongoing monitoring and evaluation are an integral part of any literacy program. As an evaluator, you should view children operating in a range of literacy contexts. This gives you a broad picture of individual children's strengths and weaknesses. Data should be gathered through day-to-day observation, work samples, anecdotal notes, Records of Reading Behaviour, formal tests, conferences with the children, discussion with other teachers, information from parents and other significant adults, and self-evaluation. Such ongoing evaluation will also help with the efficient organisation of the program and the selection of appropriate resources. Chapter 8, "Monitoring and Evaluating Children's Reading", details appropriate practises regarding reading. Chapter 9, "Writing", discusses monitoring and evaluation of writing.

With the range of information technologies increasing at a rapid rate, it is important that children are able to use technology to assist them to identify, extract, organise, analyse, synthesise, evaluate, and use information appropriately. It is also important that children learn more about how technology has influenced the lives of different people in different places at different times. Chapter 12, "Technology and Literacy", presents a practical way of introducing young children to technology processes through literature.

2 A Balanced Language Program

The key to a well-balanced language program is to give opportunities for both accessing and expressing information using different modes of language. The table below indicates six modes that can occur in any combination. For example, a class presentation of a play could involve the actors in speaking, reading, listening, presenting, and viewing. The play could involve writing and visual language as it pertains to costumes, props, and scenery. The audience would be involved in listening, viewing, and maybe an oral response.

Table 1   Language Modes

	INPUT MODE	OUTPUT MODE
ORAL LANGUAGE	**LISTENING** Accessing information from speech	**SPEAKING** Expressing information orally
WRITTEN LANGUAGE	**READING** Accessing information from print	**WRITING** Expressing information in print
VISUAL LANGUAGE	**VIEWING** Accessing information from sources other than print, e.g., maps, pictures, videos	**PRESENTING** Expressing information in visual form other than print, e.g., art, craft, charts

These modes should not be seen in isolation, and although they often go together in naturally occurring pairs, integration should be seen as paramount. For example, a class presentation of a play could involve the actors in speaking or reading their lines, listening and viewing other actors for their cues, listening and viewing the audience for their response, and presenting the overall play, including the scenery and costumes. The audience would be involved in listening, viewing, and even presenting—laughing, crying, hand clapping, and maybe talking.

In all planning, the concept of balance across the modes needs to be stressed. For instance, if you always follow the reading of a story with a written response to evaluate comprehension or enjoyment, your program is not fully balanced. Chapter 7, "Responses to Texts", gives ideas for using all language modes.

As well as maintaining a balance across language modes, it is important to provide balance within modes. Tables 2 and 3 give examples of this balance in respect of reading and writing.

**Table 2   Components of a Balanced Reading Program
The Reading Components**

READING

COMPREHENSION   DECODING

CONTROLLING THE READING PROCESS

READING FOR ENJOYMENT AND EXPERIENCE

READING FOR INFORMATION

FUNCTIONAL READING

Table 3   The Writing Components

WRITING

IDEATION   SPELLING

CONTROLLING THE WRITING PROCESS

PERSONAL PRIVATE WRITING

WRITING FOR A VARIETY OF PURPOSES AND AUDIENCES

WRITING TO ORGANISE AND EXTEND THINKING

Controlling the Reading and Writing Processes

During the first three years of school, one of your main tasks will be to ensure that children gain control over the reading and writing processes. This ensures that they will be able to comprehend and decode when reading and to formulate ideas and spell when writing. Reading and writing are complex processes with much to be learned. In order to become competent, independent readers and writers children need to control a range of strategies. They need to know how to:

- bring meaning and oral language to stories;
- use book language and structure;
- use some concepts of print;
- match one spoken word with one written word;
- move from left to right and effect return sweep;
- hear sounds in the absence of print;

- visually perceive print;
- identify alphabet letters;
- process phonological units, sound to letter/letter cluster in writing, letter/letter cluster to sound in reading;
- read and write some short high frequency/high interest words;
- use available print, people, visual, and technological resources;
- make links from the known to the unknown to solve problems in reading and writing;
- check their own reading and writing;
- self-correct their reading;
- edit their writing.

Reading for Enjoyment and Experience

As well as ensuring that children are able to read, you will want to foster a love of reading that will inspire them to read in leisure time throughout their lives. To do this, you need to expose children to a variety of genres, including picture books, poetry, adventure stories, science fiction, fantasy, biography, history, and humour, to name a few. In the first year of school, much of this will be introduced as you read aloud to your children. Discussion and activity surrounding these readings of good literature should lead children to understandings of characters, plots, themes, setting, moods, and the interactions between these different components. Such in-depth reflection helps children understand the different levels of meaning contained in many stories.

Personal Writing

In the same way as you foster a love of reading in your children, so should you foster a love of writing for it's own sake. Children should have many opportunities for personal, private writing in which they may express their thoughts and emotions, keep track of events, and come to terms with incidents beyond their control.

Reading for Information

At first, some young readers may have difficulties with the characteristics of factual genres. The text structures and language are often different from the stories they have been used to. Reading factual material also requires a different type of reading if the goal is to extract information. You may consider including narrative texts about factual topics to help children bridge the gap to the more challenging expository genres. During the first three years of school, children need to be able to:

- access appropriate information using visual, print, people, and technological resources;
- locate information in text using tables of contents, chapter headings and sub-headings, glossaries, pictures, maps, charts, diagrams, and text structures;
- extract and organise information by making notes, charts, graphs, and mind maps;
- present information in a variety of ways suitable to the topic and the audience;
- evaluate how well they controlled the process.

By introducing factual texts to children right from the start, you provide them with real learning experiences that link their classroom activities with their everyday lives outside school.

Writing for a Variety of Purposes

Just as it is important for children to be exposed to a variety of genres in reading, so is it important that children are able to express themselves in a variety of genres so that their writing is appropriate to their purpose and their audience. Examples of, and suggestions for, writing in different genres may be found in Chapter 9, "Writing".

Functional Reading

Functional reading usually requires the reader to follow some instructions and then return to the text for further instructions or information. It is the reading required by adults in order to function in society. Children can learn much about functional reading in the home as they watch parents following recipes and other written instructions. At school, this learning continues in the classroom setting through written classroom instruction, e.g., "how to" notices, Language Experience, and through reading procedural texts.

Writing to Extend and Clarify Thought

An important and often overlooked function of writing is its importance in helping children to organise and extend their thinking. This writing may be brief and is often combined with presenting, to form a mind map or semantic web. It is often used at the beginning of topics to surface prior knowledge, and during topics to organise, clarify, and extend thoughts.

3 Organisation and Management

Organisational and management skills are essential in developing a successful language classroom. These skills provide the foundation for success. In busy classrooms with many children with different needs, you can develop ways of organising the classroom to maximise every child's learning opportunities.

To start, you need to:

- be committed to a philosophy where children's individual needs are paramount;
- have a sound knowledge of the curriculum;
- take time to establish routines at the beginning of the year;
- establish attractive environments with colourful displays of children's work;
- foster positive attitudes;

- encourage children to be independent and responsible for their own learning;
- set acceptable noise levels;
- help children to devise classroom rules to promote order, harmony, and fair play;
- help children become responsible for their own classroom housekeeping;
- teach children to use classroom equipment, such as overhead projectors and tape recorders;
- devise a means of gaining attention;
- gather and organise resources to maximise their use;
- understand that language is a part of the whole day, not just reading and writing periods;
- plan a program that caters to children's individual needs and that provides opportunities for group and whole-class activities.

How Do We Do This?

One of the many things you can do, before the school year starts, is to look at *all* the reading resources available in your school and try out the following questions:

- ❏ What is available to me?
- ❏ What sort of storage and retrieval system do we have?
- ❏ Are there gaps at some levels?
- ❏ Are our resources and the way we use them managed efficiently?
- ❏ Is there an overall plan for buying new books so titles are not duplicated unnecessarily?
- ❏ Is there a lack of factual materials?
- ❏ Are there enough books at the emergent level to help my beginning readers get started?

Visit the school library and become familiar with the stock of books. How many are available to your classroom and for how long? When planning your themes for the year, you will know what resources are already in the school and which ones you will need to get from elsewhere. Make recommendations to the teacher librarian about

children's books that might be of value in your school. Does the library hold files of magazine articles and pictures that can help stimulate language use?

A good supply of art materials is essential for the development of a language program. What is your allocation for the year? Is it enough? Will you need to supplement it by finding an alternative supply? Printing businesses and paper manufacturers are often sympathetic to teachers' requirements. Learn to be a conservationist and recycle whatever you can. The children in your classroom will take their lead from your example and will provide a steady supply of resources from their homes and neighbourhoods.

Find out where filmstrips, slide projectors, overhead projectors, tape recorders, headphones, televisions, and video recorders are stored. What apparatus is available for long-term use in your classroom?

Within your classroom environment, consider the

arrangement of tables and furniture. Ensure that the library is in a comfortable, well-lit area, and that movement in and out of the classroom and between different areas is easy. Think about where art activities should take place—perhaps near the sink. Is there a large space where the whole class can gather together for stories and sharing time?

Your own preparation is vital. Some other things that you may find useful to prepare are listed below.

- Draw up name tags for your class, if learning names is difficult for you. Using a child's name from the first day on is an excellent way to establish a bond and show that you care. Spare labels, ready for unexpected enrolments, can be handy.
- Prepare several name cards for each child. Children can use them to leave on completed tasks.
- Draw up a temporary timetable to get you started in the first week. This will help you to avoid "empty moments". Plan to do too much rather than too little at this early stage.
- Prepare notices to send home with the children if you want them to bring materials or resources themselves.
- Plan an integrated language theme that the first week's classroom program can be based on. Choose a topic or an emphasis that you feel confident and enthusiastic about.
- Refer to last year's class records. Refresh your knowledge about children's development from their progress cards and individual folders containing samples of their work. Note any important points that will help you this year— but remember to keep an open mind about each child. Form your impressions as you start working together.

Classroom organisation can benefit by performing a few simple tasks.

- Prepare a calendar on which to record the weather during the first month, as a mathematics/science activity. Blank calendars for the remaining months of the year can be made later if you want to pursue this activity.
- List some classroom routines on a chart. Leave blanks for children's names as jobs are allocated.
- Make a task management board.

Task management boards

Task management boards allow children to work independently while you work with small groups or individuals. They also provide an organisational tool to help you cater to the differing needs of children in your class. Most teachers find that four instructional groups are the most that they can manage comfortably. Some, especially those teaching children in the early stages of schooling, like to see each of the groups daily; some prefer to see three groups, while others prefer to see two. It all depends on the structure you feel is appropriate for you and your class.

At the beginning of the year, you can gradually introduce optional or free-choice activities, so that children will know exactly what is expected of them. For example, if children are going to use the Listening Post or overhead projector, they will need to know how to operate these pieces of equipment. Procedures for getting, handling, and putting away books can also be explained to younger children.

The board needs to be about 60 x 90 centimetres and made of heavy cardboard, magnetic board, or similar durable material. The pull-off labels can be made of cardboard and are attached using either Velcro or magnets. Every day, you can attach the names of all the children in each group to the left-hand side of the task management board.

Use the "T" label to denote the time that a group will be working with you. Use the "O" label to denote the free-choice activity from the range of options on the right-hand side of the board.

Other labels for each group on the left-hand side of the board can indicate an activity you have set following the reading of a book, even from the previous day. This task can be designed to allow the children further time to explore a book that has been the focus of instruction, either through further reading, art, or craftwork.

As the year proceeds, you will find that children are able to take more responsibility for their own learning. This means later options can be much more flexible. The children will also have many more ongoing works, such as publishing and illustrating stories, writing book reviews, etc., so labels for these self-directed activities should then be added to the board.

Many of the resources you will be using during the year can be prepared well in advance. Some ideas for organising resources are listed below.

⊃ Make a flannel board and sets of characters from poems and stories to use with the board. Flannel boards may be made in the same way as task management boards. Keep these characters in separate plastic bags in a box, together with the flannel board.

⊃ Decorate strong cardboard boxes with coloured paper for use as group or individual reading Book Boxes. Brightly coloured, commercially produced plastic cartons may also be used.

These boxes or cartons can hold books that children have already read and books that are easy enough for them to read independently.

⊃ Prepare blank cardboard squares to use as stand-up labels for display areas. Statements about children's "finds" can be written on these.

⊃ Collect and prepare large sheets of paper for use as posters or charts. Prepare other paper for painting, drawing, and writing.

⊃ Compile a list of resources you need to get your program underway in the first month of school.

⊃ Find a strong cardboard box, cover it with vinyl contact or wallpaper, and make this your poem box. Prepare lots of appealing poems and nursery rhymes to go in it. If this is not the children's first year of school, ask their previous teacher to tell you some of their favourite verses. Include these, too.

⊃ Prepare overhead projector (OHP) transparency sheets of stories and poems for the children to use as soon as the operation of the projector has been explained. The children's own stories can be "published" for use on the OHP. The maximum number of children who may read together at the projector will need to be decided.

⊃ Make several large books with blank pages ready for use during the first weeks. A good size is 60 x 50 centimetres. Coloured paper coverings make each book more attractive.

○ Organise an attractively covered box in which children can drop in any pieces of equipment they find during the day. If a child does not know where a piece of equipment is normally stored, they can use the box. Boxes can be sorted at the end of the day.

○ Gather pencils, crayons, pastels, paints, erasers, and paste ready for use on the first day. Provide some suitable containers. Avoid glass jars because they break easily. Plastic is better suited to classroom use.

Below are a few more suggestions that can also benefit your classroom environment.

○ Collect stimulating pictures, activities, etc., that may be adapted to meet many different needs in the classroom.

○ Put up coloured paper, cardboard, or other materials on walls as backing for displays. Make sure that your display space is at a height for children that is comfortable and easy for them to read.

○ Think about where children will place unfinished work when it is time to move on to another activity. They will need name cards to identify their work clearly.

○ Put up an alphabet frieze with attractive pictures to help children identify letter and sound associations easily.

○ Arrange a display of books in the library corner of the room. Place cushions on the floor to make it an inviting place that children will want to visit.

○ Arrange storage of art supplies, paper, etc., in cupboards and on shelves easily accessible to children. Write labels so children can find what they are looking for quickly and will know where to put it away.

Suggestions for the First Week

First day

Introduce yourself to the class. Ask them to tell you about themselves. A good way to do this is to arrange the class in a circle on the floor and have a "round". Rules for rounds can be established from the start. Rules that help include the following:

- Everyone has a turn, but any individual can "pass" if he or she does not want to contribute.
- Everyone listens and gives their whole attention when someone is speaking.
- When group members finish speaking, they pass their turns on to the person sitting next to them.
- No one interrupts a speaker or asks questions until the round is completed.

Establishing rules for the classroom is important. Allowing the children to contribute their ideas to these rules encourages responsibility, too. Record ideas and rules, giving a positive emphasis to statements. Use "Walk inside the classroom" rather than "Don't run in the classroom". To ensure the smooth running of the classroom, the points listed below may need to be raised and discussed with the children.

❑ Movement about the classroom.
❑ Entering and leaving the room.
❑ Using equipment.
❑ Getting (and putting away) materials.
❑ Distributing and collecting books.
❑ What to do when visitors come.
❑ How to gain attention.
❑ What to do when work is finished or when you are busy.
❑ Classroom manners.
❑ Storing coats and bags.
❑ Setting out work, where appropriate.
❑ Arranging desks, tables, and seating.
❑ Selecting monitors.
❑ Roll-call procedures.
❑ School rules.
❑ Fire and other emergency procedures.
❑ Expectations of behaviour and work—setting standards.
❑ Where to play on the school grounds.

On the first day, begin introducing activities for your language program. Choose easy, familiar activities that need only a few simple rules. Suitable activities could include reading Big Books and poem cards, doing alphabet activities, and painting and drawing. As the week goes by, introduce a new activity each day to the whole class, making sure that every child becomes familiar with the routines associated with it.

Alternatively, you may wish to introduce a new activity to small groups while the rest of the class is occupied with other activities. Over time, as the children start to use learning centres independently, these activities become opportunities for choice rather than for directed learning. If you focus on one curriculum area each week, then at the end of the first few weeks the children can be familiar with basic learning-centre activities associated with mathematics, reading, music, language, art, and science and technology.

In the following weeks, as you are introducing and developing themes for study, you can set one or two directed activities associated with the topic for the children to do each day. This still allows plenty of free choice, investigation, and enjoyment. A theme with a science or social studies emphasis, for instance, presents an opportunity to integrate language with another curriculum area and ensures a focus on reading and writing across the curriculum.

Right from the start, ensure that there is an adequate supply of material associated with each theme for the children to read independently and for you to read with them. Have a sharing session in which you explain important things about reading materials.

- What is available?
- Where is it available?
- How many can use it? (If possible, let the children find out the desirable numbers.)
- When is it available?
- How do we use and care for materials?
- Where do we replace them?
- Who do we go to for assistance? Parents, teacher aides, librarians?
- Where do we put finished and unfinished work?

There are a number of ways to get children started on choosing activities in a language program. One way is to have a list of class names prepared with space for comments as you observe the children at work. On following days, any children that you have noticed needing assistance can be given a helping hand. You could go through the children's names, starting at a different place on the roll each day. Ask children to move quietly to their first choice of activity for the day. For group work, you could leave the choice to the children. Ask a group to choose where they are going to begin working

on an activity. Allow other groups in turn to have a choice. For less formal groups, simply ask two or three children who would like to work together to make a decision about their first choice of activity. When children, in groups or on their own, complete an activity, they can put name cards on their work before they move on to the next task.

About five minutes before the session is due to finish, give a recognisable warning signal. This allows children time to complete what they are doing and warns them not to start a new project. You will need to decide on what signal is to be used—and use it consistently. A chime bar, tambourine, drum, triangle, song, or hand-clapping rhythm could all be suitable. After sessions have finished, train the class to tidy up and insist that everyone helps. Singing a song often encourages everyone to take part willingly in the clean-up operation. Make sure there are enough rubbish bins to collect the left-overs from the morning's activities. If children find a stray piece of equipment, encourage them to place it in a designated box for sorting at the end of the day (see previous section).

Sharing time at the end of the session gives you and the children a chance to evaluate the experience. This might take place in a circle, so all children can see and hear what others are contributing. Not everyone will have the chance to share their work, but those who miss will have their turn another day. Occasionally, children can "show and tell" in small groups that give everyone the opportunity to speak. If a child has encountered a problem during the morning, he or she may want to share it so others can help find a solution. As part of your evaluation, decide if changes need to be made. Bearing in mind the children's interests and needs, ask yourself what worked or didn't work, why, and what you could do about it.

When evaluating your program, observe the children informally as they work and interact with others throughout each session. Select a few children to observe more closely and record any useful information on the class name list. Some observations might include how quickly tasks are begun or individual or group preferences for reading. You will be able to keep track of the children's progress, needs, and interests, and will be aware of how they solve problems, socialise with others, and grow in independence—all important developments. Always remember: the process is as important as the product.

During the first week

Familiarise your class with their surroundings by taking a walk around the school buildings and playground with them. You could follow this by making and discussing a ground layout of what they have seen, using boxes to represent buildings. The children could write about what they have seen or you could record their impressions for them as an individual or class effort. This activity fits in with the idea of language experience discussed in later chapters dealing with approaches and oral language.

Introduce the book you intend to use as the Shared Book for the week. Use this and language experiences as the basis for your language program until you begin evaluating progress and grouping children. Plan an activity to follow the first reading of this book and think about other activities to follow subsequent readings. In the first week, you could also read your favourite story to the class. Discuss it with them. Ask them to tell you which books they like. Use these discussions to find out their interests and include these when you are planning your program.

Other activities could include:

- recording daily weather on the calendar after class observation and discussion;
- modelling writing for the children in a class "news" book;
- recording an item of interest to everyone;
- encouraging pupils to write about themselves and to illustrate their stories;
- putting up displays of children's work—and asking them to help you organise the use of wall space.

Toward the end of the first week

Further on in the week, capitalise on the first days of classroom experience.

- Continue with the shared-book approach, following the steps outlined in Chapter 5.
- Extend the language experience introduced earlier in the week, or introduce a new language experience to motivate children to read, write, and illustrate.
- With the children, set up a learning centre in the classroom. A writing centre may be your first choice. Involve the children in deciding where it will be and what it will be stocked with. Discuss how it will be used and what your expectations are.
- Incorporate music and drama throughout sessions, where possible.
- Set up other learning centres, using the children's suggestions and planning.
- Introduce the task management board. Explain its use to the children. Gradually add more tasks for each group to accomplish, remembering to include suggestions for early finishers.
- Keep observing children at work and play. Note the children who need special assistance (e.g., speech therapy) and contact the appropriate agencies where necessary.
- Reinforce routines established on the first day. Praise children who remember and carry out the rules that have been agreed to.
- Demonstrate art skills to the children during art sessions. Give them opportunities to practise these new skills when responding to a language experience or a book during the day.

The Second Week and Beyond

Introduce a new Shared Book when you feel it is appropriate. Knowing the children better, you can plan follow-up activities that will appeal to a range of interests and abilities. Give the children opportunities for choice—and learn more about them by observing their selections, their concentration on the task, and how they cope with challenges.

Introduce new learning centres as you think they are needed, making sure that the children understand their purpose and how they are to use them effectively and independently. You will also need to change their purpose and focus from time to time to sustain the children's interest.

Continue to reinforce routines daily, assisting the children towards independence and responsibility for their own learning. They will learn that you are not always available to answer their queries. If you have taken the time to set up your program properly, they will be able to organise the materials they require and will know where to seek assistance if you are busy.

Language experiences will arise out of your theme planning and are an important part of the program. Follow these experiences with group shared writing and individual writing. There are all sorts of ways these pieces of writing can be made available for reading:

- As shared books or charts;
- As overhead projector transparencies;
- As part of wall displays;
- As published books.

This writing and display will form an important part of your language program, but it is important to keep both the program and the learning environment stimulating and challenging by introducing a new activity each day. Watch the children's interest and remove an activity if it no longer has a purpose. You should also ensure that there is an adequate supply of books associated with the theme for the children to read independently and for you to read to them.

When your routines are well established, you can begin monitoring the children's reading by taking some Records of Reading Behaviour each day. From your informal observations, select a few children and take a record while you listen to them read individually. A book they have read last year, a book from the Book Box, a shared book, or stories they have written are all suitable. As you find children on approximately the same level of reading material, you can begin grouping them. Introduce one group at a time and train them to interpret their daily program from the task management board. Don't be in a hurry to start reading groups—it is more important to establish classroom routines and management as your first priority. This patience ensures that your program will operate smoothly throughout the year.

Looking for Emergent Readers

Many teachers are unsure of when to introduce Guided Reading to acquisition readers. They are not sure how to tell if children are ready to cope with the complexities of text independently. As you watch children in a variety of literacy situations during the first four weeks, you could ask yourself the following questions:

Is the child able to:

- ❏ appreciate rhyme and alliteration?
- ❏ identify some letters and corresponding sounds?
- ❏ listen carefully to stories and make appropriate responses?
- ❏ make predictions from book illustrations?
- ❏ recognise one or two words in many different contexts, e.g., from around the room, in a shared book, on a poem card or song chart, and in their own writing?
- ❏ show that he or she knows some early concepts about print, e.g., that print tells a story, that print has directionality, that a book is held a certain way up?
- ❏ show an interest in wanting to read, e.g., often reads books in the Library Corner, Big Books, poem cards, charts, and their own stories?
- ❏ spontaneously self-correct errors made when reading shared books, language experience stories, and their own writing?

The above behaviours should arise naturally in your classroom as you provide opportunities for children to listen to stories, read Big Books, poem cards, and song charts, and record their own thoughts in writing. Chapter 6 of this book will help you to follow the procedures for these approaches.

Looking for Early and Fluency Level Readers

For children who are already reading, you will gain the information you need from Records of Reading Behaviour. As you analyse these records, you will see which cues children are using and which strategies they can control. The following chapter will assist you with the type of reading behaviours to look for and Chapter 8 gives instructions for taking, scoring, and interpreting Records of Reading Behaviour.

When your routines are well established you should regularly review the following questions on the chart below. This will help you in the decisions you make as you monitor and evaluate the effectiveness of your program.

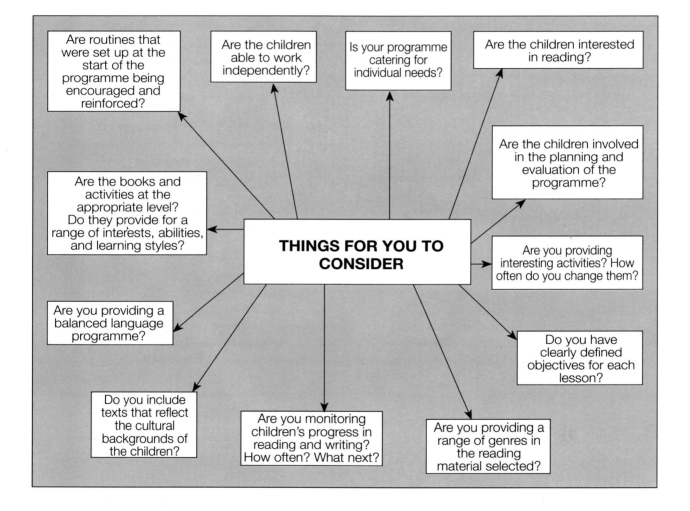

Are routines that were set up at the start of the programme being encouraged and reinforced?

Are the children able to work independently?

Is your programme catering for individual needs?

Are the children interested in reading?

Are the books and activities at the appropriate level? Do they provide for a range of interests, abilities, and learning styles?

THINGS FOR YOU TO CONSIDER

Are the children involved in the planning and evaluation of the programme?

Are you providing interesting activities? How often do you change them?

Are you providing a balanced language programme?

Do you have clearly defined objectives for each lesson?

Do you include texts that reflect the cultural backgrounds of the children?

Are you monitoring children's progress in reading and writing? How often? What next?

Are you providing a range of genres in the reading material selected?

4 Strategic Reading

What is a Strategic Reader?

A strategic reader is a reader who has control over the process of extracting meaning from a series of print cues. Such a reader is able to:

- follow the directional conventions of print;
- match spoken and written words one-to-one;
- search for and use cues from the meaning of the story, the structure of the language, and the visual and phonological information contained in the print;
- monitor their own reading behaviour by checking these cues one against the other;
- correct mistakes by taking the initiative for making the cues match;
- continue to discover new things about reading for themselves by making links from known to unknown information.

Strategies

Strategies are procedures that go on in the mind of the reader. You cannot see them, but you can infer that they are happening by observing certain behaviours.

The tables below give an indication of the strategies and behaviours for emergent, early, and fluency reading. We do not believe that there are discrete, sequential stages of reading through which all children must pass, so you should not view the acquisition of strategies as linear. At any time, you would expect to see children using a range of strategies depending on their familiarity with the text they are reading. For example, a reader is said to be at the emergent level because he or she exhibits many of the behaviours that we have grouped under this category. However, on familiar texts we would expect that child to be reading fluently and exhibiting behaviours that suggest that all the strategies are integrated. Conversely, a reader at the fluency level reading challenging text may revert to earlier behaviours, such as finger pointing.

Table 4   Strategies and Behaviours of Emergent Reading

STRATEGY	BEHAVIOUR
Directionality	Children use fingers to indicate direction and return sweep.
One-to-one Matching	Children begin to match one spoken word with one written word.
Monitoring	Children begin to notice discrepancies between the print and what they are trying to say. This may be at the level of meaning, structure, word, or letter, and may occur before an unknown word or after an error.
Searching	Children may pause and search in the picture, the print, or their memory for known information. This may occur before an unknown word or after an error.
Self-correction	Children start to correct some of their errors. This behaviour may be accompanied by the rereading of the previous phrase or sentence.

Table 5   Strategies and Behaviours of Early Reading

STRATEGY	BEHAVIOUR
Directionality and One-to-one Matching	Children begin to read the book, matching text with their eyes, but reverting to finger pointing when they are tired and/or when the text presents some new challenge that requires integration into their present repertoire of competencies.
Monitoring	Children notice discrepancies in the meaning and structure and at the word and letter levels. They use their range of known information to assist with self-correction.
Searching	Children demonstrate an ability to search using letters and letter clusters, as well as meaning and language structures.
Self-correction	Children correct many of their errors. This behaviour may be accompanied by repetition of the problem word or the preceding two or three words.

Table 6   Strategies and Behaviours of Fluency Reading

STRATEGY	BEHAVIOUR
Directionality and One-to-one Matching	Children scan phrases with the eyes. Finger pointing may occur at places of difficulty.
Monitoring, Searching, and Self-correcting	Children are able to use both large and small chunks of meaning, language structure, and visual information in an integrated way to foster ongoing monitoring of reading comprehension.

Interactions and Dialogue

The most important aspect of teaching for strategic learning is the interaction between you and the children you are helping to learn to read. These conversations should take place in the context of reading real books and will often appear to outsiders to be little more than informal chat. In fact, all the time you will be extending the children's knowledge of stories and factual material, how print works, and the process by which children become independent readers.

Your dialogue should be educational

Your conversations with children should be educational rather than managerial. A quick check of the kinds of instructions you give to children will tell you what you are doing in this area. For example, if most of what you say is along the lines of "Get your books out", "Turn to page two", "Stop talking", "Come and sit over here", or "Have you finished yet?", you may not be making the most of your opportunities.

To be educational, most of your dialogue should pertain to the book and the reading process. For instance, "What do you think this story might be about?", "Who knows another story by this author?", "Look at the picture to help you", "I like the way you read that, you made it sound so interesting", or "Yes, that word *does* look like *went*" might be more productive.

Your dialogue should build on children's strengths

There are many ways of assessing the strengths of children. Some suggestions may be found in the chapters on "Monitoring and Evaluating Reading" and "Writing". When collating your observations of children's reading and writing behaviours, couch your recommendations in positive terms.

When Anise was given a dictation from the Observation Survey (Clay, 1993) the result was as follows:

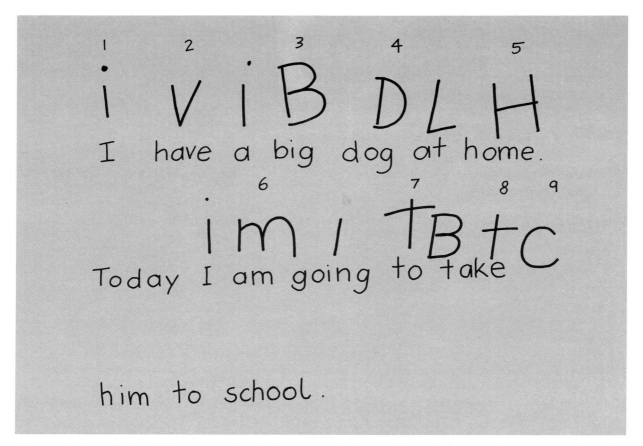

Her teacher's analysis of this task was that Anise was able to hear and record some dominant consonants and nearly knew *I*. By looking at what Anise *could* do, rather than what Anise could *not* do, her teacher was able to reinforce Anise's strengths in a positive way.

When Anise wanted to write *doll* in her story, her teacher said "You know how to start *doll*, you try it by yourself."

When Ramon was reading, his enthusiasm for the story was such that his oral language continued to override the text. His teacher praised him for the interesting way he was reading the story, but asked him to use his finger to see if he could make the written words match up with what he wanted to say.

Your dialogue should be meaningful

Effective teachers are those who engage in meaningful talk with the children both about the story and about the reading and writing processes. In most classrooms, the children will bring a variety of cultural and literacy experiences and practises to school. A skilful teacher helps each child bridge the gap and make the links between personal knowledge and the text. To do this, you will need to introduce texts to children so that they have the necessary framework and prior knowledge to negotiate and construct a meaningful experience. Samples of introductions may be found Chapter 6, "Reading Approaches". During and/or after reading, it is important that you talk to the children to help them understand the meaning of the story, comment on actions, extend the plot, bring events into personal reference, recap, resolve, and evaluate.

Your dialogue should provide specific feedback

Specific feedback is a very effective strategy because it helps children come to know what they know. You can use it to:

- Teach tasks the child does not yet control:
  "You had a really good try at that, but read it again and look a little more closely."
- Cue the child into thinking about the reading process:
  "What can you do when you come to a word you don't know?"
- Help the child to realise and articulate what he or she knows with regard to both the story and the reading process:
  "You did a good thing when you were reading that page. Do you know what it was? You realised that when you read potato crisps that something wasn't quite right, so you went back and had another try to put it right. You read chips instead of crisps the second time. How did you know it was chips and not crisps?"

Reinforce reading behaviours the child already controls:

After fluent, corrected reading — *"You read that just as though you were talking. It made it very interesting for me to listen to."*

After corrected reading —*"It was good that you went back to the beginning of the sentence when you realised that you had made a mistake. I liked the way you thought about the story in your head, then reread up to the word that caused you a problem, had a good look at the word, and the right word just popped out."*

After corrected reading when the meaning is lost —*"That looked right and we can say it that way, but try it again and think what might make sense and fit the story."*

After incorrect reading when the meaning is not lost—*"Try that again and think what would look right as well as making sense."*

Your dialogue should encourage independence

Jenny is reading *It's Noisy at Night* (Sandra Iversen, Wonder World I). She reads "It's noisy at night if the rain comes down" instead of "It's noisy at night when the rain pours." Her teacher knows that Jenny can match one-to-one. He also knows that Jenny knows *w* and the sound it makes, and can recognise *down*. To encourage Jenny to take the initiative for checking on her own reading using what she knows, her teacher merely says "Try that again."

Jules is reading *Slugs and Snails* (Colin Walker, Wonder World I). He reads "Slugs and snails are alive on dark place" instead of "Slugs and snails live in damp places." He knows something is wrong and he stops reading, hoping his teacher will help. She does. She says "You're in a muddle. What are you going to do?" Prompted by his teacher's response, Jules takes the initiative for going back to the beginning of the page and correcting his own reading.

Texts that Help Emergent, Early, and Fluency Reading

In order to help children to make secure and habituate the strategies that they will need to control increasingly complex text, you will need to be very careful in your selection of reading material—especially at the emergent and early levels. Good texts have characteristics that will help you in your choice. These features involve the suitability of subject matter, the language structures used, the illustrations, the size, amount, and placement of print, and the redundancy of information. Books in each category may be factual or fiction.

Characteristics of emergent texts

These books are often one- and two-line caption books that contain stories about subjects familiar to most children. Strong pictorial support is provided by illustrations that match the text exactly. The language patterns are predictable although the pattern can change on the last page. Sentences or phrases are contained in single lines. Short, high frequency and high interest words are used often. The print is larger than normal, positioned in the same place on each page, and provides obvious spacing between words.

Characteristics of early texts

These books contain longer sentences that may spread over more than one line or page. Many stories, though still brief, have a beginning, middle, and end. As children are now able to monitor their reading by using print cues, there is less picture support. The language patterns are not so regular and may contain rhyme and alliteration and some simple direct speech.

Characteristics of fluency texts

These books contain more pages and longer, more complex sentences about diverse subjects. Some of the concepts may be quite abstract, and the reader may be required to make inferences to comprehend the message. The illustrations tend to enhance rather than contribute to the meaning. The print may not be conventionally located on the page, and may even include direct speech in "talking bubbles" in the illustrations.

Matching categories

Although you will make your own decisions about which books are suitable for which children in your classroom, matching books to recognised levels may be helpful to you. Table 7 shows how Emergent, Early and Fluency levels match with the New Zealand Reading levels and American Basal Levels.

Table 7   Reading Levels

LEVELS	READING LEVELS		BASAL
Emergent	Magenta	1-2	Readiness
Early	Red	3-5	Pre-primer 1
	Yellow	6-8	Pre-primer 2
	Dark blue	9-11	Pre-primer 3
	Green	12-14	Primer
Fluency	Orange	15-16	1.1
	Turquoise	17-18	1.2-2.1
	Purple	19-20	2.2
	Gold	21+	Grade 3 +

Scaffolded Instruction

In any language program, you provide varying levels of support that are determined by the competencies and understandings of your children. We call this scaffolded instruction. This term implies that what children can do with help, they can ultimately do alone. To facilitate this, each child works in partnership with a more capable peer or adult who scaffolds the task by engaging in appropriate instructional interactions. These interactions can be modified in accordance with the child's increasing competence and control. These interactions are influenced not only by the child's literacy experiences, but also by their cultural and social background.

Scaffolding in the Major Approaches

At the program level, scaffolded instruction results in different approaches to teaching reading and writing. These approaches are summarised in Table 8.

Table 8   Approaches to Teaching Reading and Writing

READING	WRITING
Language experience	Language experience
Reading to children	Writing for children
Shared reading	Shared writing
Guided reading	Guided writing
Independent reading	Independent writing

While you will not be interacting directly with the children during independent reading and writing, you may have scaffolded the task by helping with the selection of appropriate material and topics prior to the children working alone.

These approaches can be represented on a continuum showing the amount of support provided.

Most Support Provided   →   →   →   →   **Least Support Provided**

Reading to Writing for	Language experience	Shared Reading Writing	Guided Reading Writing	Independent Reading Writing

Within each approach, you can further scaffold the task in the following ways:

- Through the choice of text.
- Through the amount of your input.
- Through the nature of the dialogue and interaction between you and the child.
- Through the choice of related activities.

An example of how scaffolding is provided in the major approaches to teaching reading is shown in Table 9.

Table 9   Scaffolding in the Major Approaches to Teaching Reading

LANGUAGE EXPERIENCE	READING TO CHILDREN
The child creates the story in his or her own language and provides the semantic, syntactic, and graphophonic prior knowledge that scaffolds the reading task.	The teacher scaffolds the task by taking responsibility for all the decoding and much of the meaning. In this way, the teacher fosters the growth of children's appreciation of book language, story structures, and depths of meaning.
SHARED READING	**GUIDED READING**
The teacher takes responsibility for decoding and provides a scaffold to the language structures and vocabulary, allowing the children to focus on meaning. Second and subsequent readings pass the decoding task over to the children.	The teacher scaffolds the task through the introduction and the support afforded during reading. This varies depending on the background of the children and the complexity of the text.

Table 10   Scaffolding in the Major Approaches to Teaching Writing

LANGUAGE EXPERIENCE	WRITING FOR CHILDREN
The child brings the meaning gained from an experience and expresses it in his/her own language. The teacher assists by providing the amount of support needed by an individual, group, or class in the writing component of the lesson.	The teacher scaffolds the task by taking responsibility for all the encoding and much of the development of various skills and understandings of the writing process. In this way the teacher demonstrates the finer points of writing for beginning as well as more accomplished writers.
SHARED WRITING	**GUIDED WRITING**
The teacher takes responsibility for some of the encoding and provides a scaffold for the concepts of print and spelling and provides models of different children's messages. Over time more of the writing is able to be handed over to the children.	The task is scaffolded by the teacher to each child's needs in the writing of ideas, words, and sentences, while the children are engaged in writing their stories.

Because your aim is to produce independent learners, you will need to be constantly:

- varying your approach;
- choosing appropriate material;
- modifying your dialogue;
- choosing activities that allow for revision, reflection, consolidation, and extension;
- encouraging children to take responsibility for what they know, and to apply this to new learning;
- promoting independence.

To assist you with the complexities of providing powerful instruction within each approach, we have included examples of the changing nature of scaffolding in Guided Reading.

Table 11   Guided Reading with Emergent Readers

BEFORE READING	
Choice of text	Choose a text that presents a balance between that which is familiar and challenges that can be met with support.
Teacher support	Surface prior knowledge without reference to the book. Introduce the book in two sentences to familiarise children with the theme, the plot, the setting, and the characters. Give the children the opportunity to hear unfamiliar vocabulary and language structures that they will not be able to solve in any other way.
Dialogue	Discuss the pictures in the entire book with the children. Allow the children to read the whole book at their own pace as independently as possible.

DURING READING	
Teacher support	Check for evidence of understanding of directionality, one-to-one matching, monitoring, searching, and self-correction behaviour.
Dialogue	Use questioning that refers to reading process. For example, "What do you do when you come to a word you don't know?" Give specific feedback for appropriate processing behaviour. For example, "It was good to see you matching each word you said with a word in the story."

AFTER READING	
Dialogue	Discuss children's responses to the text for enjoyment and understanding.
Teacher support	Demonstrate parts of the reading process, if necessary. For example, "When you come to a word you don't know, this is what I want you to do. Go back to the beginning of the sentence, look at the picture, and think about the story in your head. When you get to the word you don't know, look at it closely for something you know and try to say the word."
Choice of activities	Choose activities that revise, consolidate, enhance, or extend.

Table 12   Guided Reading with Early Readers

BEFORE READING	
Choice of text	Choose a text that presents a balance between that which is familiar and that which presents a challenge.
Dialogue	Discuss the title and predict what the story may be about, clarifying prior knowledge if necessary. Discuss the pictures in the book to get the sense of the story, but note that the children are now more able to confirm or revise their predictions by integrating cues from print.

DURING READING	
Teacher support	Check for evidence of monitoring, searching, and self-correcting behaviour. Check to see that children are using their current competencies to solve text problems. Check to see that at problem points children are taking the responsibility for checking sources of information using all cues.
Dialogue	Discuss explicit information contained in the text. Questions may refer to the reading process at points of difficulty.

AFTER READING	
Dialogue	Elicit the children's responses to the text. Deepen understandings through implicit questioning (i.e., questions that require answers based on textual information and prior knowledge).
Teacher support	Demonstrate parts of the process, if necessary.
Choice of activities	Choose activities that revise, consolidate, enhance, or extend.

Table 13   Guided Reading with Fluency Readers

BEFORE READING	
Choice of text	Choose a text or a selection of texts that the children can read with 90% accuracy or more.
Teacher support and dialogue	Guide reasons for reading the text. Elicit predictions if fiction or content if factual.

DURING READING	
Teacher support and dialogue	For fiction, guide the children toward understanding of the story and the language used, the theme, the setting, the plot, and the characters. For factual books, assist children to access the relevant information.

AFTER READING	
Teacher support and dialogue	Discuss responses to the story. Extend and deepen the meaning.
Choice of activities	Choose activities that revise, consolidate, enhance, or extend.

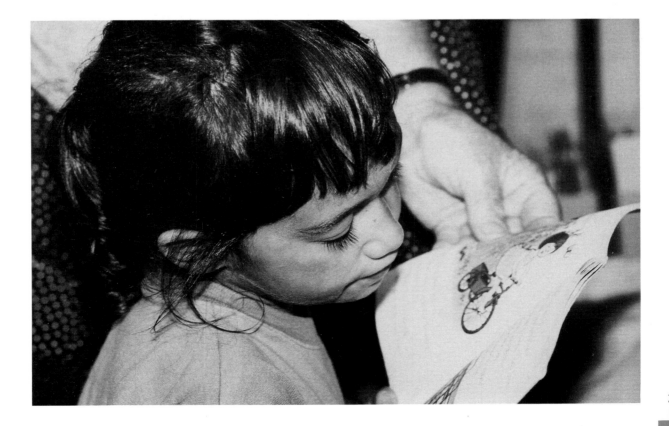

6 Reading Approaches

Reading to Children

Studies from emerging literacy perspectives have shown us that the children most able to take advantage of formal literacy education are those who have been read to a lot in their preschool years.

Why read to children every day?

Reading to children is fun, simple, and cheap—and as such, it is the most effective advertisement for reading. Many children learn to read, but never become regular readers because they see no purpose in it. Children *need t*o see a purpose in reading. If you believe that you learn to read by reading, you must learn to *want* to read. Reading to children, therefore, models both the "how" and "why" of reading.

Reading to children every day imparts new understandings, too.

- It leads to an understanding of characters, themes, and plots, and the relationships between them.
- It leads to an understanding of the sequential and connected nature of books.
- It leads to an understanding of the conventions of printed matter.
- It imparts new information, as well as enabling children to interpret their own world and a world that may be distant in time, place, and imagination.

In terms of language skills, reading to children leads to vocabulary acquisition. Listening comprehension precedes reading comprehension. If children have never heard a word before, they will not use it in their vocabulary and therefore will not be able to read or write it. Experience and research shows the most effective way to increase the vocabulary of eight- and nine-year-olds is to read to them.

Before reading a book, you can help your class activate their prior knowledge so that they are able to make links between what they already know and the new information they are receiving. Your questioning and discussion during and after the reading of a book will help their understanding of the structure, setting, plot, sequence, characterisation, and the values of the story. This will enable them to interpret what they are reading or hearing and allow them to make their own intellectual and/or emotional responses to the author's message. Reading quality literature in your classroom will enhance your program and introduce interesting ideas and language to your children.

The patterns and rhythms found in books can be introduced to children in an enjoyable way. Reading to children exposes them to language structures, aspects of good grammar, and the ability to use book language. Good teachers can also use reading sessions to encourage some decoding skills.

When should you read to children?

Every day for at least fifteen minutes.

What sort of books should you read to children aged five to seven years?

Any good literature that is full of rich, descriptive vocabulary can be read to children. In choosing books, you might want to consider other questions, too.

- ❏ Does the book avoid stereotyping class, culture, or gender?
- ❏ Is the book at least three or four grades above the children's reading level?
- ❏ Will the book be relevant to the children or help them interpret their own world?
- ❏ Does the book kindle curiosity and spark imagination?
- ❏ Am I reading books that cover a range of different genres, including both fiction and factual, prose, and poetry?

Language Experience

The earlier comments about the organisation and management of your language program included suggestions about using Language Experiences as an introductory approach, either to the whole program or to individual activities, such as a Shared Book or the Guided Reading of a book. Language experiences give children the prior knowledge they need to make sense of the text they are reading.

How can we define Language Experience?

Language experience is a technique for helping children explore, understand, talk, write, and read about their social and physical environment. It provides opportunities for expressing observations, feelings, and ideas, thus encompassing both rational and emotional responses.

Language experience is a technique that helps children to think logically, arrange ideas, solve problems, and draw conclusions.

Language experience is a procedure for helping establish clearly perceived links between the real world and the symbols of language. The child comes to realise that thoughts can be talked about, written about, and read about. Through reading, these thoughts can be shared with others.

Why should I include Language Experience in my program?

Language experience provides:

- a link between oral and written messages;
- reciprocal gains in reading, writing, and speaking;
- experiences in all modes of language;
- learning about concepts related to printed material (that print contains a message, that these messages are assembled in a consistent order of letters within words, of lines on a page, of pages in a book, of punctuation, and of the appropriate use of upper case and lower case letters);
- a valid method of reading instruction focusing on ideas rather than words, so children develop the habit of searching for meaning;
- an opportunity for you to separate and focus on individual reading skills, such as left-to-right directionality, one-to-one matching, monitoring, predicting, checking, confirming, and self-correcting.

It capitalises on children's fascination with language and language patterns and encourages the use of creative language. Language experience gives children an opportunity to express feelings, release tensions, and cope with fears. Opportunities can be presented for using existing language structures and building in new language structures, and a variety of different registers can be used for recording. Registers might include descriptions, narratives, poems, reports, or recounts.

Language experience allows for perceptive observation and expression of ideas. Language structures are open for experimentation, and new vocabulary can be clarified and consolidated. Differing presentations of similar language or information can also be examined. These facets, as well as being valuable in themselves, also introduce children to good writing habits. Language experience may also help children understand the book conventions of title, author, illustrator, layout, and page sequence.

The procedure for Language Experience

Begin planning the experience by noting the outcomes you want to achieve. Collect the resources you will need—for the experience itself, for recording it, for displaying it, and for further creative responses to the experience. Children's creative responses could come in the form of box models, mobiles, paintings, wire models, sketches, or papier mâché construction, for instance. Make sure the materials are on hand.

Devise the activities. Experiences could take the following forms:

Talking
- As a whole class, in small groups, or individually;
- In a formal debate or by taking turns;
- Informally, where children talk freely, question, and answer.

Writing

- Alone, in pairs, in small groups, or as a whole class;
- By dictating to you or to another child;
- Using the child's own language in an innovation, a report, a recounting, as a poem, or a description, or on a chart;

Presenting

- By "publishing" in some form.

Reading

- By you, the child, or shared with a group or the class;
- Directed or free choice;
- A book, a chart, a wall story, or reading on tape, or as part of a wall display, or a combination of these.

Work should be displayed because its value is then easily apparent. As well as wall stories or murals, try OHP transparencies, charts, audiotapes, or videotapes. In book form, work can be displayed in large and small books, concertina (accordion) books, diaries, and class newspapers.

It is important to provide time to revisit the experience and also to evaluate it. You might ask yourself if the experience lead to improved oral and written language and improved reading ability. The children's evaluation could take the form of questions such as "Did I enjoy this experience?" or "Did I learn something new?" or "Did I take part to the best of my ability?"

A Language Experience example

The following is a sample experience based on the theme "cats". This Language Experience would provide an introduction to a Shared Book lesson.

By the end of the lesson, the children should be able to:

- Talk about the experience of observing a cat or cats;
- Write about the experience using vocabulary and ideas formulated during the class discussion;
- Read their own and/or the class's written language about the experience.

These are the learning outcomes you should be seeking.

Prior to this lesson, you will need to write a poem on a card in enlarged print about a cat. The traditional rhyme *I Love Little Pussy* is used here. You may have a favourite that you would prefer to use. If practical, arrange to have a docile cat brought to the classroom for the children to observe.

Talk

Seat the children in a circle and begin the lesson by reading the rhyme to the group. Invite the children to read along with you.

> I love little Pussy,
> Her coat is so warm,
> And if I don't hurt her she'll do me no harm.
> So I'll not pull her tail nor drive her away,
> But Pussy and I very gently will play.

After the reading, this poem can be added to the class Poem Box for further enjoyment at other times.

Introduce the cat into the circle. Say to the children "This is my cat and it is paying a visit to our classroom today. We are going to observe it very closely and I would like you to sit very still while we do this so that it doesn't become frightened." Ask the children to tell you about the cat. Discuss its colour, size, shape, texture, features, and the sounds and movements it makes. Some key questions might be:

- What do you think my cat's name is? What would be a good name for it?
- What colours can you see in its fur?
- What colour are its eyes?
- How would you describe the shape of its ears/eyes/tail/paws?
- What does its fur feel like?
- How do you feel when you stroke its fur?
- Why do you think it is swishing its tail?
- Can you think of interesting words to describe the way it feels or moves?

Accept all the children's ideas, making sure that they explore their ideas further.

When you have removed the cat from the classroom, allow the children to experience the ways that cats move about. Ask children to act out the ways a cat sleeps, stretches, creeps, prowls, leaps, and growls. Investigate the association of feelings with movement, for example, an angry cat arching its back, a sleepy cat stretching and yawning.

Write

Brainstorm descriptive words and ideas with the group. Record the words and ideas on a chart. You can expand these ideas into a written sequence on a chart or in the form of a wall story.

Mrs Depree brought her cat to school today and it sat on the floor with us. At first, it looked scared of us, but after a while it seemed to get used to everyone looking at it.
Its name is Smoky because it is a grey and white cat. James thought that it should be called Fluffy. James said it was the fluffiest, furriest cat he had ever seen!
Smoky scampered around the floor chasing little bits of paper and it let Lucy give it a cuddle. Then it bit her and made her cry!
Then Smoky got tired and went to sleep on Nicky's lap and we could hear it purring very loudly. Mrs Depree put it back in its basket and put it in the staffroom. We think Smoky liked being with us and will be lonely when it wakes up.

At other times, you may want the children to write their own versions of the Language Experience. Use the same procedure. The only difference is that the children do the writing instead of you.

Read

Read through the class story together, asking the children to suggest any improvements or additions to your first draft. Ask the children to help you to decide which sentences should go on each page of the book or wall story you are going to prepare for them. Encourage them to think up a title for the book.

Then ask them to draw pictures to illustrate each page. While they are doing this, you can write the story in enlarged print on the pages. Paste the pictures into the book with the children watching you as you do so.

Now everyone will be ready and eager to read their own class book about the Language Experience they had. You will find that the books you make from these experiences will be very popular reading if you make them readily available for the children to use.

Shared Reading

Shared Reading is fundamentally an extension of the "bedtime story". As a reading methodology set in a non-competitive learning environment, risk-taking, mistakes, and approximations are seen as a normal part of learning—not signs of failure.

Shared Reading is a step between reading *to* children and independent reading *by* children—the step where children learn to read by reading. Successful Shared Reading allows the reader to take over this task gradually, rather than all at once.

Through Shared Reading, all children can become independent in reading material that would otherwise be too difficult. It is a reading methodology that allows less-able readers to function as readers.

Why should I include Shared Reading in my language program?

Shared experiences in language are part of the heritage of all cultures. Shared Reading can be used with any age level or ability, any class group, or individual. It develops positive feelings towards stories and book experiences in a relaxed, secure situation.

Shared Reading can be an important part of your language program because it:

- allows for, but does not demand, active participation;
- allows children to learn at their own rates;
- helps children to be independent with material that would otherwise be too hard;
- eases book resource problems for you and your colleagues;
- enables you to use exciting literature, full of rich language, in a program for beginning readers;
- enables you to set a snappy pace within and across lessons.

Shared Reading can also help teaching within the context of actual reading. There are a number of teaching points of which you can take advantage:

- Aspects of language, such as structure, rhyme, rhythm, and alliteration.
- Concepts about print, such as directionality, spatial concepts, punctuation, words, and letters.
- Clarification of concepts, such as whole story, or individual words.
- Reading strategies, such as predicting, locating, checking, confirming, and self-correcting at the levels of letter, word, and full text.
- Information skills, gained from things such as the title, author, illustrator, publisher, index, glossary, and table of contents.
- Extension of both sight and listening vocabulary.

Shared Reading has been found to be very valuable in teaching children who speak English as a second language. Research shows that, in less than a year, children are reading with greater comprehension, know more sight words, and are better able to repeat simple English structures orally. The new language is learned in a situation where motivation is high.

The procedures for Shared Reading

Make sure that the children are sitting close to you and the book. Is everyone able to see the text and the pictures? For the first reading, you should have the only copy.

To motivate children, begin with a general introduction. Open the book completely so that the children can see the front and back covers at the same time. Read the story with a few pauses to invite predictions from the children. Accept all responses positively. If the story is repetitive, be pleased if the children join in—but do not demand this. A slight pause is often sufficient to encourage them.

At the end of the reading, discuss personal responses to the book. You may want to record some of these responses on a chart to refer back to, after the book has become familiar. You can then compare children's responses and feelings at a later stage with what they thought earlier.

Second reading

Use an enlarged text, an overhead projector, or multiple copies of the book. Read the story again, encouraging the children to join in. Encourage further discussion of colourful phrases. Invite the children to experiment with intonation and expression.

Attend to teaching points as they arise. These will be determined by the objectives of the lesson, and may include:

- clarification and extension of the understanding of the story as a whole;
- clarification, location, and extension of vocabulary;
- checking of language predictions—did guesses make sense, sound right, look right?;
- concepts of print.

Try to extend the children's thinking and "tune in" to the author's intentions. Ask questions such as "Why do you think that happened?" and "How would you feel?" You may tackle some teaching points during the reading and some at the end.

Always keep the meaning paramount and never try to squeeze too much out of a book—there will be many other opportunities to teach with other books.

Further readings

For some children, two readings will be sufficient for them to reread the book independently. Others may need further reading with you, with more capable peers, or with a tape of the story. The large text and at least one small copy should be available for readers to return to in their own time.

Follow-up activities can elicit children's responses to the story, and may include a variety of reading, speaking, writing, dramatic, and art activities.

Shared Reading books for emergent and early readers

Before selecting a text for Shared Reading, ask yourself these questions:

- ❏ Does the book have impact, charm, magic, and excitement?
- ❏ Does the book have a good plot and provide for the broadening of insights?
- ❏ Does the story development lead the children to participate in problem solving?
- ❏ Does the book have interesting pictures that develop and support the story line?
- ❏ Is the sentence structure appropriate or so awkward that it may get in the way of fluent reading?
- ❏ Does the story have repetitive elements? Does it have a cumulative pattern? Does it recur in a cycle around a series of events?
- ❏ Will this story stand up to numerous rereadings?
- ❏ Is this story too simplistic or too rigidly matched to the group/class ability?

Sample Shared Reading lesson

The following is a sample Shared Reading lesson which would follow on from the Language Experience lesson described previously. The sample book used is *What Do I See in the Garden?* (Helen Depree, Wonder World I).

By the end of the following sequence of lessons, the children should be able to:

- relate some aspect of the stories to their own lives;
- predict some vocabulary, using the meaning, structural, and visual cues of the story;
- discuss their feelings with each other about the animal characters and the events in the story;
- read the whole book, or parts of it, independently.

These are the learning outcomes you should be seeking.

The first reading
Orientation to the book may include a short poem about cats or birds or a Language Experience lesson. Then, show children the cover of the book. Open it completely and tell them the title, author, and illustrator. Say "This is a story about a cat and a bird who live in a garden."

Check the children's prior knowledge of cats and birds by asking questions such as, "Do any of you have a cat or a bird at home?" and "What can you tell us about them?" Quickly sketch semantic webs on charts to record their answers.

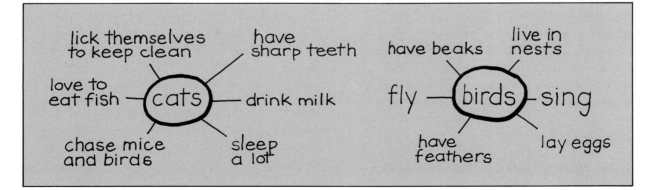

Read the book to the children, getting them to guess what might be happening in the pictures on the first two pages, and then check their predictions as they listen to the story. Read with as few interruptions as possible, pausing only to clarify meaning if necessary.

Discuss the story with the children to extend their enjoyment and understanding. Ask questions such as these:

"Did the story end the way you thought it would?"
"How did the bird feel when it flew away?"
"How did the cat feel when the bird flew away?"

Refer back to the semantic webs to compare the actions of the cat and bird in the story with the information recorded on the charts.

After this first reading of the story, the children in one trial class role-played the actions of the cat and bird while the teacher played a tape of the text. Sound effects and music were added to the tape to heighten the tension as the tale progressed. Then the children drew pictures to illustrate the sequence of the story. These pictures were used to make an enlarged version of the book for use in the next reading of the story. The teacher wrote the text on a word processor, making sure that the text format was the same as the original.

Adapt the above activity to your own class, aiming to end up with a Big Book of the children's own making.

The next reading

Show the children the original book before introducing the Big Book made by the class. Invite the children to read along with you as you point to the words in the text. After the reading, encourage discussion of the rhyming parts of the text (e.g., sleeping, peeping, etc.). Ask "What other words do we know that start like this word *cat?* Do we know anyone whose name starts with the letter *c?*" Some questions may be asked during the reading and some afterward, but remember not to spoil the enjoyment of the story.

Further readings

Some children will be able to read the book independently by now and others will still need the support of you and others as they read. Both versions of the book should be left where the children can have access to them during the day. The story can also be available at the Listening Post and parts of the story can be written out on cards and illustrated by the children. These cards can be read by the children independently or in pairs. Ultimately, all the cards could be placed in the sequence of the story.

When the children are familiar with the structure of the story, an innovated version can be made and shared.

What do I see in the bedroom?
What do I see in the bedroom?
    Baby sleeping.
    Baby peeping.
That's what see in the bedroom.

What do I see in the bedroom?
What do I see in the bedroom?
    Baby thinking.
    Baby blinking.
That's what I see in the bedroom.

Shared Reading for early readers — an example

This sample lesson uses *Shadows* (Marie Stuttard, Wonder World I) as a Shared Book. Other books using descriptive, lyrical language can also be used.

By the end of the following sequence of lessons, the children should be able to:

- move appropriately to a given word;
- classify words according to movement, rhyme, and alliteration;
- write words to show movement;
- write a cinquain using descriptive words.

These are the learning outcomes you should be seeking.

Shadows could be incorporated into an integrated science/language unit on shadows or may be used solely for the beauty of its language. The following Shared Reading experience focuses on the language aspect of the text and uses science activities as optional extension work.

Introduction

Introduce the book by saying something about its contents and outlining an activity. For example, say "Today we are going to read a book that is filled with lots of interesting-sounding words that tell about how different shadows move. It also has a rhythm and lots of rhyme. Before we read it, we are going to go out into the playground to see how our shadows move. Then we are going to play a guessing game."

Take the children into the playground and allow them to move freely, watching their own and other children's shadows. After a period of free movement, introduce some specific movements that they will meet later when you read the book (e.g., wriggle, gallop, prance). If your children do not use English as their first language, you may have to demonstrate the movement. Allow fifteen to twenty minutes for this movement, exploration, and observation and then seat the children in a circle in the playground. Say "I want you to think in your head of some words that tell how your shadow moves. When you have thought of one, I want you to fold your arms so I will know you are ready to play the game."

Choose one child to demonstrate the word they have thought of. The rest of the class have to guess the word. When a child gets it right, record the word on a piece of card. That child then demonstrates their movement.

Collect about fifteen examples, or more if time allows. Record each example on a separate card. Return to the classroom and read *Shadows* to the children. Make sure you hold it up so all children can view the pictures and the text.

The second reading

Use OHP transparencies that you have made of the book. Read the story again to the children, asking them to join in with rhyming words where possible. Hesitate before such words to allow them to participate. You may also need to enunciate the initial sound to cue them in (e.g., "Shadows can wriggle and waggle and *tumble*, Shadows can ramble and scramble and *st...*").

Reread the words you wrote on the cards previously and see if the children can supply and demonstrate more from the book. Write cards for these also. Use these words where you can in normal conversation during the day—"You can march out to lunch now" or "Scramble around the room and pick up the paper."

Further readings

On the third day, try the third and fourth readings. Half the class reads the text with you while the other half performs the appropriate actions. Change over. Add any further movement words onto separate cards.

Sit the children in a circle and ask them to classify the words using set rings or Hula Hoops. Accept any classifications the children may offer, such as all the words that are fast movements, all the words that make you fall over, all the words starting with *s*, or all the words ending with *le*. Encourage children to look for larger chunks of print that are similar. Read these words together and note that they look and sound the same—but that their meanings are different. Perform the movements to show different meanings.

You may wish to make several sets of the words and allow the children to work independently in small, mixed-ability groups, with a friend, or individually. Children can work at classifying words in different ways or playing word games:

"I'm looking at a word that starts with *s*, and it tells how a mouse moves."
"I'm looking at a word that ends with *emble*. It tells what you do if you're cold or frightened."

On day four, reread the story from the OHP transparency. Children will be taking most of the control of the reading at this stage. Discuss how the children could write words to show movement. For example:

Ask children to write their words using coloured pens and display the results as a mobile.

On the fifth and sixth days, demonstrate writing a cinquain using movement words.

Shadows
dance, prance,
march, leapfrog, jive,
ramble, scramble, tumble, stumble
Shadows

Ask children to write their own cinquains and to make shadow puppets from black cardboard

attached to thin sticks. Children can read their cinquains to the rest of the class, illustrating the movements with their shadow puppets.

Other extension activities at this stage could include making a shadow mural with captions, writing individual shadow stories, performing a shadow hand-jive (with moving hands), making shadow shapes on the wall, measuring shadows at different times of the day, and reading other books to find out how shadows are formed.

Guided Reading

What is Guided Reading?

Guided Reading is an approach to reading instruction that allows children to demonstrate their control over text. It leads them to understand that reading is a process of actively reconstructing an author's meaning.

From your point of view, Guided Reading enables the grouping of children with similar needs so that the task is neither too easy nor too difficult for anyone. It allows you to assist children to predict their way through the text, then check, confirm and, if necessary, correct those predictions themselves.

Why Guided Reading?

There are several positive benefits from Guided Reading:

- It helps deepen and widen understanding of the text.
- It presents many opportunities for specific teaching in context as necessary.
- It encourages silent reading.
- It allows you to cater more accurately to children's needs by grouping children of similar ability together.

Preparing for Guided Reading

Ability groupings can be determined from Records of Reading Behaviour. Groups of five to six are preferable, certainly no larger than eight.

Select a text at the children's instructional level (90-94%) accuracy. Remember that children are active problem-solvers—they expect to meet challenges in reading, but also expect to surmount

them. Too many problems will lead to a decline in interest. Consider the choice of text carefully, as difficulties may lie in the concepts, the language structures, or the vocabulary. You will need one copy of the text for each child.

Select the purpose for reading

At emergent and early levels, as well as focusing on the meaning, your emphasis will be on strategies required to read the text. These strategies are one-to-one matching, directionality, locating known words, predicting, monitoring, searching, checking, self-correcting, and fluency. The integration of all cue sources and strategies is vital.

Reading the text

You can observe the reading behaviour of each child if they are seated near you. Before giving each child in the group a copy of the text, you can discuss the ideas contained in the story. This ensures the children have this knowledge before they attempt to read the book.

At the emergent level, this will include you summarising the theme and the plot in one sentence, then opening the book and talking the children through the pictures. Do not read the book to the children or you will take away their opportunity to solve problems in new text.

At the early level, you and the children can discuss the ideas contained in the title and the plot. If the topic of the new book is unfamiliar to the children, then you can do a Language Experience lesson before introducing the book—this builds prior knowledge for them. For example, if the children have never been to a zoo, a visit could be arranged before reading a book about zoo animals.

Give each child a copy of the text. Until one-to-one matching has been established, the children should be asked to use a finger to help the reading. Once this behaviour is secure, children should be encouraged to let their eyes do the work and only return to finger pointing when they need extra support on difficult material. The children then read the text independently. You may stop them to deepen their understanding, ask questions, or focus on a teaching point that is an objective for the lesson. Keep interruptions to a minimum, so as not to interfere with fluency and meaning. Above all, avoid round-robin reading.

Responding to the text

At the conclusion of the reading, allow time for children to respond to the story and for you to clarify any further teaching points. The Guided Reading lesson need not be followed with any set activity. Should you wish, you could try asking the children to reread the story to themselves or a friend. Children could also respond to the story through writing, drama, and art. This may be teacher- or child-directed.

The book may be taken home that night for reading to a parent and returned to school next day. One copy may then be placed in the group Book Box for independent reading. This rereading of the book provides the practice on known texts that beginning readers need.

Guided Reading for emergent readers — an example

This sample lesson uses the book *Basketball* (Sandra Iversen, Wonder World I). By the end of the following sequence of lessons, the children should be able to:

- locate the title, author, and illustrator on the cover and title page;
- read the text independently using pictures to help meaning;
- match one spoken word with one written word when reading, using a finger;
- take some initiative for self-monitoring if either meaning or one-to-one matching breaks down.

These are the learning outcomes you should be seeking.

Introduction and reading

Use this lesson plan with small groups of children with similar abilities. Start by saying, "Today I have brought a basketball to see how many things we can do with it. We will all have a turn and see how many different things we can do. Who would like to start?" Guide the children to different activities, including those in the book, such as running, passing, and catching. When each child has had a turn, return them to a semicircle on the mat and show them the book *Basketball*. Hold the book up so that everyone can see it clearly.

Say "This is a book about basketball. It tells us the sorts of things that players do in a basketball game. Lots of things they do are the same as the things you just did. Who can come and point to the title? The author's name is Sandra Iversen, and that means she wrote the story. The person who drew the pictures is called the illustrator, and his name is Bernard Dobbie." Point to the author and illustrator credits on the cover as you say this. Repeat the procedure with the title page, asking the children to join in.

Show the children the illustrations, page by page, unfolding the story as you go. "This page shows us all the people who have come to watch the basketball match. The girls in the front are cheerleaders. They have come to cheer their team along. Who can tell me something else about cheerleaders?" Accept all responses and extend understanding orally and through role-playing. Look at the next picture and say "Now the players are running." Turn to the next page and ask "Who can tell me what Number 11 (point to the player) is doing? That's right, he's bouncing the ball. He's going bounce, bounce, bounce, isn't he?" Turn to the next picture and ask "Now what is he doing? I wonder if Number 12 will catch it?" Children will respond as you turn the page. Say "Yes, he did catch it, and now he's jumping in the air as he shoots for goal and... (turn to last page) ...Slam dunk, in it goes! That'll be two points. Now the other team will get the ball and see if they can run and bounce and pass it to their end of the court and score. It's a fast, exciting game, isn't it?"

Close your copy of the book and hand the children individual copies. Say "Point to the title. Let's read the title together. Turn to the title page. Let's read the title together again. Now turn to where we are going to start reading the story and put your finger on the first word we are going to read. Remember, every time you read a word you are going to point to it with your finger. Let's read the story now."

Children will start reading the story together—and some will soon get ahead of others. You will need to move among the children, helping them individually to match the spoken and written words. Reinforce appropriate reading behaviour with comments such as "I liked the way you noticed that you ran out of words and started again and made them match" or "I liked the way you checked with the picture when you weren't sure what the story said." After all the children have finished, extend the meaning further if necessary. If you decide to include a follow-up activity, any of the following would be appropriate:

- Get children to re-read the story to themselves or a friend.
- Make a Language Experience wall story about the role-playing at the beginning of the lesson. You write the captions and the children illustrate them using crayon and watercolours.
- Make a mural of the basketball game. Children can draw and cut out characters and you can write the captions.
- Go outside and play basketball. The children in the reading group could show the rest of the class how to play.

Give each child a copy of the book to take home to read again that night.

Guided Reading for early readers — an example

This sample lesson uses *The Wind* (Helen Depree, Wonder World I). By the end of this session, the children should be able to:

- solve any difficulties in the text by using letters and letter clusters, as well as meaning and language structures;
- respond to the onomatopoeia of language and make up new combinations;
- read the story independently.

These are the learning outcomes you should be seeking.

This book could be introduced as part of an integrated science/language study of weather. A windy day would be ideal to introduce this book. Begin by sharing a poem about the wind. Then take the children outside to stand still in the wind. Ask "What can you feel? What can you see? What can you hear?" Suggest that the children run around in the wind. Then ask "How did it feel when you ran into the wind? How did it feel when the wind was behind you?"

Back inside, seat the children in a semicircle on the mat. Talk about their experiences outside. List their responses on a chart.

What We See	Windy Day Feelings	How Wind Helps Us
Trees blowing over	We run around feeling silly	Windmills make power
Branches snap off	I laugh a lot	It dries out clothes
Hair blows everywhere	It makes Dad mad	It blows yachts along

Say to the children, "Today we are going to read this story about the wind. The author is Helen Depree, and the pictures are by Julie McCormack. Let's look at the pictures and see if we can see some of the things we saw when we were outside." Accept all contributions. Say "The words at the beginning of each sentence describe the action that is happening on each page. These words help make the story more interesting." You may need to demonstrate how you would work out the words *crickle-crackle* on the first page to help children get underway.

Observe children carefully to see if they are searching and self-correcting. Are the children taking responsibility for checking information using all cues? The children should be asking themselves what sounds right, what makes sense, and what letters they expect to see. Provide for early finishers by asking them to think about other windy-day events that might have happened and other word combinations that could be used, such as snippy-snappy, slippy-sloppy, chirry-whirry, etc.

After reading, you could ask some of the following questions:

"What words were used to describe the movement of the branches? Could we use other words?" (Write these on strips of paper to paste on a windy day mural created by the children)
"What words were used to describe the movement of the flags? Do you notice anything about these words—*flitter, flutter, flags?*"
"Can you think of any other words that begin the same way?"
"Which words are the describing words on each page?"

For extension activities some suggestions you could choose from are:

- make the book available in the group's Book Box;
- provide other books and poems about the wind for the children to read;
- compile information about the wind on charts, on wall stories, or in books;
- write a group poem about the wind;
- create a "windy day" mural using pictures drawn and cut out by the children and the describing words contributed by the children, written on strips of paper to paste on the mural.

Guided Reading for fluency readers — an example

This sample lesson uses *Jack de Pert at the Supermarket* (Carolyn Heke, Wonder World I). By the end of this lesson, children will be able to:

- relate some aspect of the story to their own lives;
- discuss ways in which family members help each other;
- predict, eliminate, scan, check, and confirm text when reading silently;
- read to locate specific information in the text.

These are the learning outcomes you should be seeking.

Book orientation
Begin with a discussion about being part of a family and the ways in which family members help each other. Give a copy of the book to each child, saying "This is a book about a father and his son, Jack, who go shopping together. Read the title and

see if that tells us where they are going shopping."

If there are second-language learners in the group, it would be helpful to visit a local supermarket or to make a hamburger before reading this book to "scaffold" the task for them.

Ask the children "What sort of things can we get at a supermarket?" and list their ideas. Create a chart with the following questions and ask children to think about them while they are reading.

"What do you think Jack and his father are going to buy?"
"Dad keeps asking Jack what they need to buy. Why does he do this?"
"When you get to the bottom of page 7, see if you can guess what they can make with all the things that they have bought."

While the children are reading the book, you should be observing them and helping children who are having difficulties. For example, if a child comes to a word they don't know, such as *bring*, suggest that they leave the word out and read on to the end of the sentence before starting again. If that doesn't solve the difficulty, ask "What do you know that might help you?" If necessary, ask "Do you know another word that starts like this one?" The child might say "Breakfast." Respond by saying "Yes, it does start the same way. Look at the rest of the word. What other words do you know that end with those three letters?" The child might say "Thing." Usually, they will then be able to put the two parts together to discover what the word is. If the difficult word is a long one, such as *refrigerator*, and it cannot be worked out from context, model how a word can be broken into syllables. Ask "What useful parts or chunks of this word do we know from other words?"

It is helpful to provide something meaningful for early finishers to do, such as reading other books or poems related to this topic. They can also write down words to describe Dad and Jack. List these words under "Dad" and "Jack" headings. Children could suggest some other ingredients used to make hamburgers.

When everyone has finished reading the book, discuss the questions on the chart. Ask other questions, too.

"Do you think that Jack had decided he wanted to

get Dad to buy all the ingredients for making hamburgers *before* he went to the supermarket?" "How would you describe Dad as a person?" "How would you describe Jack as a person?"

Ask the early finishers to say how they described Dad and Jack. What do others in the group think?

Follow-up activities
As follow-up activities, children could do the following:

- Write a recipe for making a favourite hamburger.
- Prepare a shopping list of ingredients that would be needed to make a chocolate cake, a fruit salad, or a pizza.
- Think of words to describe a hamburger. These can be recorded by you on cards with Velcro backing to stick onto a large picture of a hamburger.
- Prepare pencil sketches of themselves eating their own hamburger. They can paint large pictures from their sketches during an art session.

Independent Reading

What is Independent Reading?

Independent Reading occurs when a child, on their own, reads material that does not require the assistance of a more competent peer or adult. This reading may be teacher-directed or selected by the child. It allows children to practice and extend newly acquired reading competencies, and provides for the "boot-strapping" effect of reading and learning to read.

Independent reading also:

- allows children to select books from areas of personal interest;
- frees you to work with small groups or individuals;
- allows children to work at their own pace.

The following are three Independent Reading approaches.

Individual Reading

The focus of this approach is that each child will have an individually tailored program.

Procedure
Select a wide variety of books at the children's independent reading level (95-100% accuracy). At the emergent and early stages, much of a child's independent reading will occur with books that have been previously read in a Guided or Shared Reading situation. Familiarise yourself with the books and prepare the children by discussing ways of organising, recording, selecting, and sharing.

Steps in this approach include:

- introducing the method of recording;
- helping children learn how to select appropriate books;
- explaining some appropriate activities for sharing, such as reading a favourite part, retelling a story, comparing two books, showing and discussing illustrations, sharing extension activities, or "selling" a book;
- introducing some extension activities;
- explaining conferences;
- "selling" some books yourself to the class.

Individualised Reading

The individualised program is the same for any group of children, but children are free to move through the program at their own pace.

Procedure
- Devise programs for children working at a similar ability level.
- Collect resources.
- Decide on follow-up activities.
- Write a "contract" for children to follow.
- Explain the contract to the children.
- Take a short time each day to check with children and sort out any problems that may have arisen.
- Have a group sharing time and/or individual conferences during the course of the program.

Sustained Silent Reading

Set aside a time daily for uninterrupted silent reading. This time could be about five to ten minutes, depending on class level. Ask children to select a book or books prior to the session, and allow them to read without interruption. It is very important that you model interest in, and enjoyment of, reading for children at this time.

Using a Single Book in Different Ways

We have made the assumption that you will be selecting texts to suit the needs and abilities of your children and that you will be planning reading/language learning outcomes as well as content area outcomes. In this way you are able to use the same book for children with different competencies depending on the approach you take and the amount of support you provide. The following example shows how to use the same book, *Every Shape and Size* (Colin Walker, Wonder World I), for reading to children, Shared Reading, and Guided Reading.

The animals depicted in the illustrations are Page 3: Diplodocus, Coelophysis; Pages 4, 5: Brachiosaurus; Page 6: Triceratops, Plesiosaurs (in water); Page 7: Plesiosaurs (in water), Pteranodon (flying); Page 8: Stegosaurus, Compsognathus; Page 9: Tyrannosaurus; Page 10: Triceratops, Apatosaurus; Page 11: Ornitholestes, Plateosaurus. You should note that animals such as plesiosaurs (water-dwellers) and pterosaurs (flying reptiles) are not technically classified as dinosaurs (which only lived on land). They are prehistoric reptiles, as are dinosaurs, but they are not dinosaurs—just as a lion and a zebra are both mammals but not the same animals.

Introduction for all approaches

Find out what children already know about dinosaurs and other prehistoric reptiles. Say "This is a story that tells us some facts about dinosaurs. What facts do we already know?"

On separate cards, list the facts that children give. When all facts are recorded, sit the children in a circle on the floor and spread the fact cards in front of them. Use large set rings or Hula Hoops to help children classify the facts and choose a suitable label for each group (e.g., dinosaur names, dinosaur food, shapes and sizes). Write these labels on cardboard and add them to the rings.

Ask "What else would you like to know about dinosaurs?" Record questions on a chart:

> **What We Would Like to Know About Dinosaurs**
> Where did dinosaurs live?
> Why did they all die?
> Which were the biggest dinosaurs?

Say "Let's read this book for two purposes. First, let's see if our questions are answered by this book and, secondly, let's see if we find out something in this book that we hadn't thought to ask."

At this point, depending on the ability level of the children, you may choose to:

- read the story to the children;
- share the story with the children;
- guide the children towards independent reading;
- give individual copies to the children to read independently.

Reading to children

Use this approach for a whole class or mixed-ability groups at the emergent level. Hold the book so that all the children can see the text and the illustrations. Read the title and ask the children what sort of dinosaur facts they now expect to learn from this book. Read the story to the children, and stop after "Some dinosaurs were enormous." Ask "Who can tell me the name of this dinosaur?" Accept all responses and reinforce the correct one after all children who choose to have had a chance to respond.

Continue the story, stopping once more to identify a well-known animal. After reading, say "This book told us a lot about dinosaurs, didn't it? What things did it tell us that we already knew?" Accept all answers.

Refer back to the illustrations and name any dinosaurs or other reptiles that have not yet been identified. Ask "Did the book answer any of our questions?" If it did, record responses next to the questions on the chart. Discuss what you have discovered and suggest reading other dinosaur books if the questions weren't answered. What new facts were learned that hadn't been asked about?

Ask children to choose one or more follow-up activities:

- Look for other dinosaur books to answer your questions.
- Write one dinosaur fact from the book and illustrate it.
- Make a large dinosaur mural, with dictated captions for each drawing.
- Draw and cut out dinosaurs. Group them using set rings or Hula Hoops. Categories could include meat-eaters, plant-eaters, bigger than our classroom, smaller than our classroom, etc.

Shared Reading

For whole-class or group reading at the emergent level, follow the above lesson plan until you get to follow-up activities. For the follow-up activity, have children draw and cut out dinosaurs and other prehistoric reptiles to illustrate a large copy of the book. You should write the text on each page exactly as it appears in the printed version.

On day two, the second reading is used to recap what was learned from the book previously. Using the large book and a pointer, reread the story to the children, encouraging them to join in where possible. Point out repetitive language structures, as on page 3. This helps the children to predict the language structure used in the book. After reading, reinforce dinosaur names and observe one dinosaur closely. Ask children to describe the dinosaur orally for you to record, adding any other facts that children know about the dinosaur:

"A stegosaurus was smaller than a tyrannosaurus, and bigger than a pterodactyl. Stegosaurus had a small head and plates on its back. Stegosaurus ate leaves."

Follow the same procedure with four or five dinosaurs, and then get children to work in small groups making collage pictures to illustrate the descriptions.

By the third reading, many children will be able to read most of the large text with little assistance. After reading, look at the illustrations closely to see what the land looked like when the dinosaurs were alive. List the similarities and differences with today on a chart. In subsequent readings, children can return to either the large or the small copy of the book to read independently or with a more capable friend. Allow time for this follow-up reading and a choice of activities, such as looking at other dinosaur books, reading dinosaur poems, illustrating their own or other people's dinosaur facts, building dinosaurs using construction blocks or models, or writing and illustrating their own dinosaur descriptions.

Guided Reading

Use this approach for children reading at an early level or with small groups of similar ability. With everyone having their own individual copy of the book, introduce it to ensure that the children have prior knowledge of the meaning and the language structures they need to produce when prompted by the print cues. Say "This is a non-fiction story that tells us about dinosaurs. It tells us some general facts about dinosaurs and compares them to each other. It is called *Every Shape and Size*. Let's look at the pictures together and see if we can decide what facts the book might tell us."

Turn to page 2 and say "The book starts and ends by telling us that dinosaurs no longer exist and no one really knows why they all died. Can anyone tell me a word that means there are no dinosaurs alive any more?" Accept all responses and clarify, if necessary. Say "The book goes on to compare some dinosaurs with others. It compares size on the next two pages." Allow children to comment as they look at the pictures.

Turn to page 6 and say "I wonder what the book is telling us on these two pages?" Encourage the children to predict using the pictures, but discourage them from trying to read the print at this stage. You want them to have the complete picture in their heads before they start to integrate the visual information. Turn to page 8 and say "These pages tell us about dinosaur food." On page 10, say "Now we're describing dinosaurs. I wonder what facts the book might tell us? Look at the pictures and describe a dinosaur to me." Allow children time to look at the illustrations closely and offer some descriptions. Agree or disagree as appropriate, and extend where necessary:

"Yes, some dinosaurs certainly are showing their teeth. I wonder if it's the meat-eaters who have big teeth like that?"
""I can see the one with spikes, too. They look really sharp, don't they? What else could we call those spikes?"
"Yes, some do walk on two legs. What other animals do you know that walk on two legs?"

Turn to the last page and say "I wonder why all the dinosaurs disappeared?" Accept all responses, and close your book. Say "I want you to read the book yourself now. What will you do if you come to a word you don't know?" Accept all answers and continue.

"That's right. You will go back to the beginning of the sentence, think about the story in your head, read the sentence again, and when you come to the word you don't know you'll think about what you know that might help you. This might be the picture, what you want to say, or something about the word that you know. Try what you think it might be, then check to make sure it makes sense, sounds right, and looks right."

The children should then all start to read the book individually at their own pace. You should observe children as they read, noting what they do when they reach an unknown word or after an error. You may need to move among the children offering individual assistance where required.

Children who finish before the others may:

- read the book again to a friend;
- look at the illustrations in more detail to see what the land was like in those days;
- name as many dinosaurs and other reptiles as they can in the book.

When everyone has completed reading, discuss what the book told them that they already knew and which facts were new to them. List synonyms for some words, such as *enormous*. Discuss any words that most children found difficult. Write *could* and have children generate other words that rhyme. Write these underneath and alert children to the rhyming chunk of the word.

Follow-up activities may include reading more dinosaur books and/or poems, making write-your-own dinosaur books, painting and describing one of the dinosaurs, or listing some dinosaur facts. Allow children to take the book home for the night to read to a caregiver and to be returned the next day. One of the copies can be put in the Book Box for future independent reading, and the other copies returned to the central storage area for other teachers to use.

7 Responses to Texts

The following ideas are suggestions for meaningful activities that children can carry out independently while you are working with a small group. It may be advisable to introduce all of the activities over a period of time, e.g., the first six weeks of the school year, to the whole class before getting children to undertake the tasks on their own or in groups. This ensures that children understand the procedures and will have acquired the necessary group interaction skills beforehand. Some of the activities are more appropriate for use with the whole class, some for groups, as more support from you may be needed.

Frequently during these follow-up activities, the children will be working together, discussing their ideas, and planning what needs to be done. This spoken interaction is vital in helping the children to develop their skills in oral language and to bring meaning to reading and writing tasks. They may also share any of their responses to reading by telling others about their work in a sharing time at the end of the session.

When planning activities to follow the reading of a book, remember that children learn to read by reading and that the activities you plan should enhance the experience and increase learning opportunities. Often, Guided Reading followed by Independent Reading of the book by the child is sufficient. Choose one or any of the activities that may be suitable for your classroom:

Activities

- Read other books about the same topic or by the same author.
- Retell a story—orally, or through role-playing, written language, or using puppets.
- Respond to a book through painting and drawing.
- Read a story on overhead transparencies.
- Retell a story using silhouette shapes of characters on an OHP or magnetic board.
- Collect poems, jokes, and riddles about a book topic to make a group or class book.
- Tell or write a different ending for a story.
- Engage in paired or "buddy" reading.
- Listen to and read along with a story at the Listening Post.
- Make up a play about a story.
- Make up innovative stories based on language patterns encountered in a story.
- Illustrate or tell a friend about a particular event in a story.
- Draw and cut out a favourite character in a story and write a description of this character.
- Draw pictures to show the sequence of a story.
- Make a map to show all the places visited by the characters in a story.
- Match pictures with sentences describing the event in a story.
- Arrange sentences in sequence and read.
- Make a collection of cut-out characters from a story to mount on a painted background for a wall mural and write and add descriptive captions.
- Make a Big Book or wall story of a book.
- Make a diorama or peepshow of a scene from a story (a shoe box can be used for this).
- Read from Book Boxes.
- Go on a reading walk around the classroom, reading the wall displays.
- Read poems from the Poem Box.
- Engage in alphabet activities, such as using magnetic letters and manipulative alphabet cards to make words and sentences.
- Create an illustrated time line of events in a story.
- Think of word associations following on from a word in a story.
- Use mime and movement to describe words in a story.
- Make graphs related to a story where appropriate.
- Role-play a story without a script.
- Create semantic webs before and after reading a book.
- Make a "Wanted" poster for a character in a book.
- Play book title charades.
- Make a mask of a character in a book and use the mask in a play.
- Write an imaginary letter between two characters in a book.
- Make illustrated bookmarks showing a scene or characters from a book.

- Write a television commercial advertising a book and act it out.
- Describe a favourite character to others.
- Recite poems or read rhyming texts and clap the pattern.
- Discuss with others how to follow a recipe, construct a model, play a game, etc.

Responses to Literature

Many of the above suggestions to follow Shared or Guided Reading of a text are appropriate to follow the children's reading of good literature. You could also consider introducing some of these ideas after you have read a book to the class. Remember that it isn't always necessary to ask the children to make a written or artistic response to a book. Often the enjoyment and discussion of the story is enough..

However, we can also use literature to teach children how to make inferences, how ideas can be interpreted from different points of view, and how conclusions can be drawn from the information given in a story. When we ask children to think about the meaning of the text and demonstrate the process by which we reach an understanding of what has been read, we are helping them to acquire literacy skills for lifelong learning. They will then be able to apply these skills across the curriculum. Below are some graphic outlines for assisting children to organise their ideas after listening to a story.

These charts were used in one class as a follow up to listening to a story. The teacher had involved the children in a lot of discussion prior to recording their ideas on paper.

Character outline

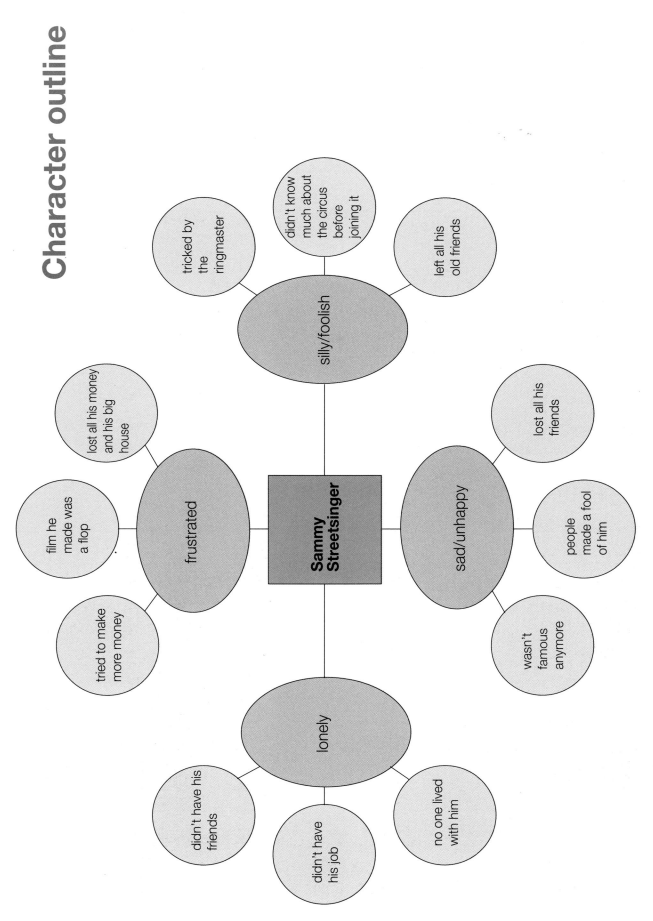

Sammy Streetsinger

silly/foolish
- tricked by the ringmaster
- didn't know much about the circus before joining it
- left all his old friends

frustrated
- lost all his money and his big house
- film he made was a flop
- tried to make more money

sad/unhappy
- lost all his friends
- people made a fool of him
- wasn't famous anymore

lonely
- didn't have his friends
- didn't have his job
- no one lived with him

Story Chart for **The Boy Who Loved the Rain**

Written by **Barbara Haupt (Published by North/South Bks, New York 1991)**

Where the story takes place:

In a town with a marketplace.

Characters in the story:

Florino
young boy
merry
thoughtful
musical

Lisbeth
magical
old woman
helpful
kind

What happened:

People in the town didn't like the rain. Florino came along. Lisbeth showed him how to make tunes with the raindrops. Florino made up different tunes. The people were cheered by the music.

The problem:

The people were miserable when it rained.

The solution:

Florino collected raindrops to make tunes which made them happy.

What the story is really about:

That people can be helped to see good in things.

Values brought out in the story:

trust respect truth
                kindness

Descriptive language used:

pelting rain; tingling melody; grumbling crowd; miserable people; quick as a lightning flash; her smile was magical; pushing the dark clouds aside.

STORY OUTLINE FOR John Brown, Rose and the Midnight Cat

Author:

Jenny Wagner

Publisher:

Kestrel Books UK 1977
Bradbury Press. Inc.
USA 1978

Date:

13. October 1993

Setting/Main Characters:

Rose's house and garden. Rose. John Brown. The Midnight Cat

The Problem:

John Brown wanted Rose all to himself. He was jealous of the Midnight Cat.

Sequence of the story:

John Brown lived happily with Rose. He kept her company all the year round.

One night Rose saw something in the garden but John Brown wouldn't look at it.

Later, John went outside and drew a line around the house. He told the Midnight cat to stay away.

Rose started to put out milk for the midnight cat but John Brown would sneak out to tip the milk out.

Rose got sick and told John Brown that she was going to stay in bed forever. John Brown thought hard about that.

John Brown let the midnight cat into the house which made Rose happy again.

The solution to the problem:

John Brown was sad to see Rose sick and he let the cat into the house to make her feel better again.

Story Theme:

What the story is about:
John Brown didn't want his life changed. He was jealous of the cat.

The point of the story:

You aren't happy when you are jealous.

Venn Diagram to Compare and Contrast the Stories

Too much Noise .... and It Could Always be Worse

Different   Alike   Different

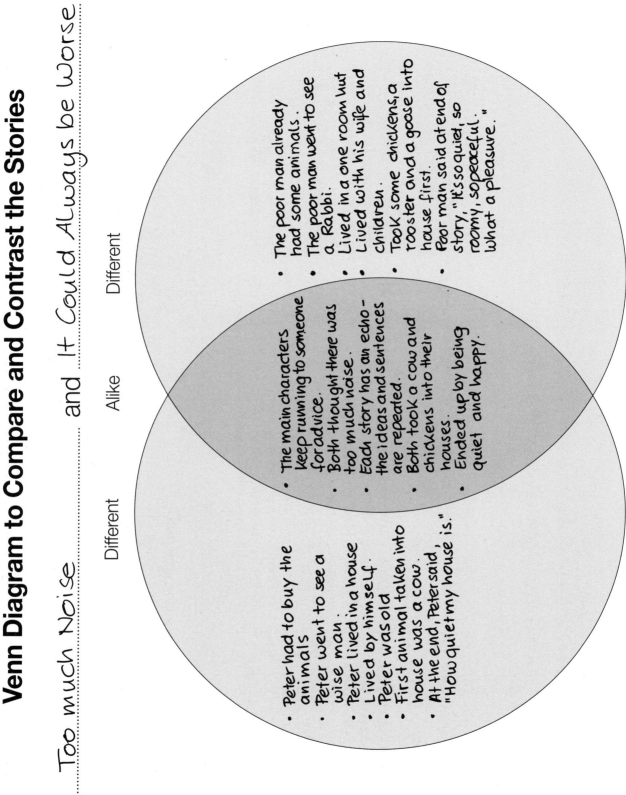

Too much Noise (Different):
- Peter had to buy the animals
- Peter went to see a wise man.
- Peter lived in a house
- Lived by himself.
- Peter was old
- First animal taken into house was a cow.
- At the end, Peter said, "How quiet my house is."

Alike:
- The main characters keep running to someone for advice.
- Both thought there was too much noise.
- Each story has an echo – the ideas and sentences are repeated.
- Both took a cow and chickens into their houses.
- Ended up by being quiet and happy.

It Could Always be Worse (Different):
- The poor man already had some animals.
- The poor man went to see a Rabbi.
- Lived in a one room hut
- Lived with his wife and children.
- Took some chickens, a rooster and a goose into house first.
- Poor man said at end of story, "It's so quiet, so roomy, so peaceful. What a pleasure."

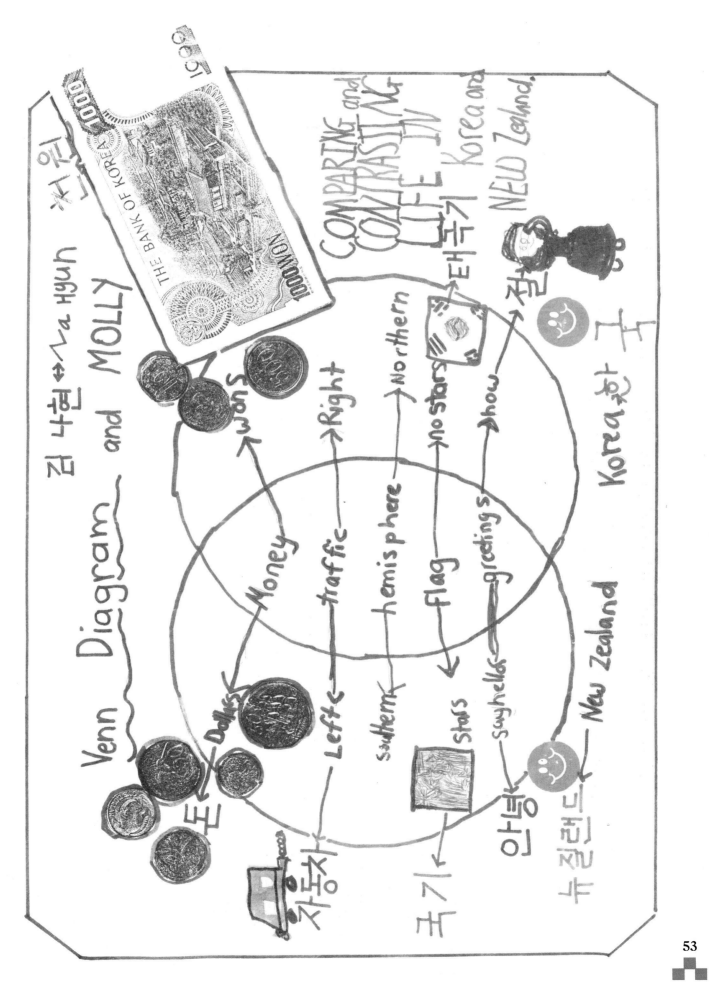

Venn Diagram

김나현 ↔ a hyun and MOLLY

COMPARING and CONTRASTING LIFE IN Korea and NEW Zealand.

태극기 정

Korea 환 국

Seasons
Right
Northern
no stars
show

Money
traffic
hemisphere
Flag
greetings
Dollars
Left
southern
Stars
Say hello

자동차
크기
Stars
안녕
New Zealand
뉴질랜드

THE BANK OF KOREA 1000 WON
1000
1988

The Venn Diagram on the previous page was initiated quite independently by two children during a class study of a Social Studies topic. They had been previously introduced to this method of presenting information in the comparison and contrasting of the stories *Too Much Noise* and *It Could Always Be Worse*. This example illustrates the ability of seven-year-olds to transfer prior knowledge to a new situation.

Blank charts for your children to work with are in the Appendix.

8 Monitoring and Evaluating Children's Reading

Making Progress

The most useful way of monitoring reading progress and getting a true picture of both what a child can do at a particular point in time, and what a child has learned to do over a period of time is to take a Record of Reading Behaviour. From such a record you can gain information on the children's control of the reading process as evidenced by their ability to search for and use cues from the meaning, the structure, and the visual and phonological information, and also the children's use of strategies such as monitoring, searching, and self correction.

The Record of Reading Behaviour

The Record of Reading Behaviour is based on the work of Marie Clay and Kenneth Goodman who pioneered the concept of close observation of children's behaviour, especially as it relates to the type of miscues children make as they read.

Steps for taking the record and analysing the record

1   Selecting the text
The text you choose for the record will depend on your purpose. For instance if you want to see how well the child is reading at his or her current instructional level, you will choose a book that the child has already read. If you want to see if the child is able to cope with more difficult material, you will choose a book from the current instructional level that the child has not seen before.

2   Introducing the text
Children should be given an introduction to any text that they are being asked to read to help them make sense of the author's message. Before taking a record on a story that the child has read before, you may need to do no more than introduce the text by supplying the title. If the child is unfamiliar with the book, you should give the child the title and a one- or two-sentence summary of the plot and theme. For example, "This is a story called *Buster McCluster*. It's about a man who planted some sprouts and didn't watch for bugs. When he cooked them, all the bugs popped out and gave his wife a fright." If the story contains any particularly difficult syntax or vocabulary, some account of these should be incorporated in your introduction.

3   Taking the record
Choose a passage of 100 to 150 words (unless the entire book contains fewer words). Sit the child beside you so that you can see the text. Some teachers like to photocopy the text so that they can make notations on a copy of the text. If using photocopies, be careful not to get into the habit of fitting the child to the text you have photocopied, rather than using material that is appropriate to the child. Where children are experiencing difficulties, it is easier to record their efforts on a blank Record of Reading Behaviour, rather than be constrained by the small space afforded by a photocopy of the text.

After your introduction, the child should read the text independently. You must resist all temptations to teach while you are taking the record, as any intervention except telling the child an unknown word will distort the interpretation of the record. You need to remember that you are looking closely at what the children can do by themselves.

While the child reads the text, you use the suggested notations to record all the reading behaviours the child exhibits.

✓✓✓✓✓   correct reading

✓✓✓✓ shop/store   miscue

✓✓✓ big/— ✓   insertion

✓✓✓ —/not ✓✓   omission

✓✓✓✓R✓   repeats one word

✓✓✓✓R✓   repeats phrase

✓✓✓ shop|SC / store| self corrects

✓✓✓ store|A   appeals for help

✓✓✓ store|T   teacher tells

The *A appeal* and the *T told* often go together like this:

✓✓✓✓ store|A|T

It is important that you allow enough wait time to give the child a chance to work on a problem before telling, but also important that you do not wait so long that the child loses the meaning of the story while trying to solve the unknown word. A neutral comment in such an instance to help keep the process going is to say to the child "You try it."

Very occasionally you may need to tell a child to "Try that again." This instruction is confined to instances where the child is way off track and in great difficulty and has no chance of regaining the meaning without help. For example:

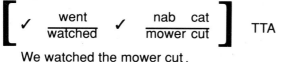

We watched the mower cut.

Place square brackets around the text causing difficulty and ask the child to read that passage again. All the text in the square brackets is then scored as only one error and the new response from the child is scored in the usual fashion. For example:

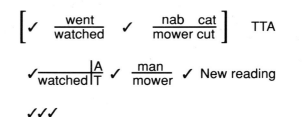

✓ watched|A|T ✓ man/mower ✓ New reading

✓✓✓

We watched the mower cut the tall grass.

At points of error, always note the child's response on top and the text below. While you are learning, use a pencil, space the check marks well while still matching them to the number of words in the line, and write down as much as possible of what the child says. You can always fill in the text later. You may also wish to tape the reading for further reference. As you become more proficient with your observations, you will notice more and more behaviours. Practice is the key to success.

4   Retelling the story

To check the child's level of comprehension in relation to the plot, the setting, the characters, and any underlying inferences, you should invite the child to retell the story in his or own words when they have completed the reading. You may need to follow this retelling with questions to elicit further information.

5   Calculating the reading level and the self-correction rate

The purpose of calculating the reading level is to tell you if the book is at a level at which the child can read independently, or with guidance, or if it is at a level which will merely frustrate the child. An accuracy score of 95-100% suggests that the child is able to read this and any material of similar difficulty easily and independently. The purpose of calculating the self-correction rate is to give you some guidance as to how well the child is able to both notice and correct errors during reading.

An accuracy score of 90-94% suggests that this text and texts at a similar level will present challenges that the child will be increasingly able to control with your guidance in an instructional reading situation.

An accuracy score of less than 89% suggests that the material you have chosen is too hard for the child to control alone and that you should use such material in a Shared Reading situation or that you should read it to the child.

6 Scoring the record

Substitutions, insertions, omissions, and teacher-told responses score as errors. Repetitions are not scored as errors. Corrected responses are scored as self-corrections.

These is no penalty for attempts that end in a correct response:

w w went
  went

Multiple, unsuccessful attempts at a word score as one error only:

will we when
    went

If there are alternative ways of scoring, credit the child with the fewest errors. The lowest score for any page is zero.

If a child omits a line or lines, each word omitted is counted as an error. If the child omits a page, deduct the number of words omitted from the number of words that you have used for the record. If the child repeatedly makes an error with a proper noun (the name of a person or a place), count this as an error the first time only. All other incorrect responses count as errors each time.

Paul
Peter if repeated five times counts as one error.

looks
looked if repeated five times counts as five errors.

Pronunciation differences are not counted as reading errors unless accompanied by incorrect locating responses.

7 Calculating the reading level

Note the number of errors made on each line on the Record of Reading Behaviour in the column marked E. Total the number of errors in the text and divide this into the number of words that the child has read. This will give you an error rate. For example, if the child read 100 words and made 10 errors, the error rate would be 1 in 10. Convert this to an accuracy percentage using the Error Rate/Accuracy Percentage Table in the Appendix, and fill in the appropriate box on the Record of Reading Behaviour.

8 Calculating the self-correction rate

Note the number of self-corrections in each line in the column marked SC on the Record of Reading Behaviour, and total them. Add the number of errors to the number of self-corrections and divide by the number of self-corrections. For example, if the child makes 10 errors and 5 self-corrections:

$$\frac{10 + 5}{5} = \frac{15}{5} \text{ or } 1:3$$

Thus for every 15 errors made, 5 were corrected, which gives a self-correction rate of 1 in 3. Or put another way, the child corrected 1 of every 3 errors made. A self-correction rate of 1 in 3 to 1 in 5 is considered good, and tells you that the child is not only noticing, but is able to do something about discrepancies while reading.

9 Analysing the record

The purpose of analysing the Record of Reading Behaviour is to enable you to draw together a picture of reading behaviour related to the processes involved in getting meaning from print. From this analysis, you can adjust and monitor your teaching program.

Analysis of the reading record can be broken down into eight steps.

i   For each error and self-correction, read the sentence up to the point of error and ask yourself what led the child to make this mistake. Try to determine if the child was using cues from the meaning (semantics), the structure of the language (syntax), the visual information contained in the print (graphophonics), or a combination of these.

ii For each self-correction, ask yourself what led the child to correct this error.

iii Look to see which cue(s) the child uses predominantly. As you analyse each child's subsequent records, you will see patterns emerging that show you how well the child is integrating cues.

iv Look at the child's behaviour at an unknown word. Does the child make no attempt, seek your help, reread, read on, or make some attempt using one or more of the cues? Circle the predominant behavour on the Record of Reading Behaviour.

v   Follow the same procedure to see what the child typically does after an error. Circle the predominant behaviour.

vi If the child is still reading at the emergent level, note directionality and one-to-one matching behaviours.

vii Note the child's understanding of, and

memory for, the characters, setting, plot, and inferences. The ability to retell at least three-quarters of the story, either unaided or in response to your questions, is considered adequate.

viii Draw all this information together and use it to guide your teaching focus for this child.

There can be several outcomes from this analysis.

You may like to take a more balanced approach to the teaching of reading. If you find that most of your children exhibit only the same narrow range of strategies when reading text independently, it may suggest that the focus of your teaching has been on these, rather than a wider, more balanced approach.

A certain strategy might become the focus of a class or group shared-book experience. For example, you may find that you have had to tell some of the children many of the words in the text. During your next shared-book lesson, you will be able to model effective strategies for figuring out unknown words.

A group of children at different stages of reading acquisition, who have a common need, could be formed. For example, you may find that some children are reading in a stilted, word-by-word manner. You can draw these children from across a range of reading abilities to give them extra practice in reading fluently.

You could institute different teaching emphases for children reading at the same level of difficulty. The following two completed Records of Reading Behaviour show children reading the same text using different strategies to solve their reading problems. They will each need a different teaching approach. The text they worked from follows:

Rico lived in a big city
And he ran a flower shop.
Rico loved his flowers
for the flowers were very quiet
And Rico loved quiet.
But the city where Rico lived
was not quiet.
If he saw a car or bus, Rico yelled,
"Quiet! Why can't you be quiet?"
Then he said to himself,
"Rico you don't like this city.
Why don't you move away?"
But Rico didn't move out of the city.

RECORD OF READING BEHAVIOUR

Name:	John
Age:	
Date:	5 / 6 / 93

Title:	Colours	
Series:	MᵃᶜMillan	(Seen)
Stage:	1:2	Unseen

Calculations

Error Rate $\frac{RW}{E}$ = 1: $\frac{75}{17}$ 1:4

Accuracy % 75%

S/C Rate $\frac{(E + SC)}{SC}$ = 1:

Level: Easy   Instr   (Hard)

Understanding from Retelling/Questioning

Characters	Yes	........✓........	No
Setting	Yes	....	(No)
Plot	Yes	....	(No)
Inferences	Yes	....	(No)

Competencies (circle predominant behaviours)

(1 on 1 matching)   (Directionality)   (Fluent Reading)

At an unknown word

Makes no attempt	Seeks help	Reruns	Reads on
Attempts using	(Letter/sound knowledge)	Meaning	Syntax

After an error

(Ignores)	Seeks help	Reruns	Attempts s/c
Self-corrects using	Letter/sound knowledge	Meaning	Syntax

Rio and the Red Pony	E	SC	E msv	SC msv
✓ ✓ ✓ ✓ Country/city	1		ⓜⓢⓥ	
✓ ✓ ✓ ✓ ✓ ✓				
✓ lived/loved has/his ✓	2		ⓜⓢⓥ / m s ⓥ	
✓ ✓ ✓ when where/were ✓ quick/quiet	2		m s ⓥ / m s ⓥ / m ⓢⓥ	
✓ ✓ lived/loved quick/quiet	2		m ⓢⓥ / m s ⓥ	
✓ ✓ country/city were/where ✓ ✓	2		ⓜⓢⓥ / m s ⓥ	
✓ ✓ quick/quiet	1		m ⓢⓥ	
✓ ✓ ✓ ✓ ✓ ✓ ✓ ✓				
Quick/Quiet R ✓ ✓ ✓ quick/quiet	2		m ⓢⓥ / m ⓢⓥ	

59

	E	SC	E msv	SC msv
✔ ✔ ✔ ✔ ✔ ✔ ✔ <u>do not</u> ✔ <u>his</u> <u>country</u> 　　　don't　　　this　　city	3		Ⓜ ⓢ Ⓥ m ⓢ Ⓥ	
✔ <u>didn't</u> ✔ ✔ 　don't	1		Ⓜ ⓢ Ⓥ Ⓜ ⓢ Ⓥ	
✔ ✔ ✔ ✔ ✔ ✔ <u>country</u> 　　　　　　　city	1		Ⓜ ⓢ Ⓥ	
	17			
TOTAL				

John had already seen this story and read it very fluently. He read unknown words using his letter sound knowledge, and failed to stop and check on his reading even when it didn't make sense. From the retelling, it was evident that he had gained only a moderate understanding of the characters and was unable to talk about the setting, the plot, or make any inferences. His accuracy was 75%. John needs a program that equips him with strategies that will enable him to keep on track. He needs to know how to search for and use cues and how to monitor and correct his reading. His teacher's prompts will be directed towards encouraging him to take responsibility for detecting his errors and putting them right. She will do this through questions that require John to check to see if what he has read makes sense and sounds right, as well as looking right. She may explicitly model such a behaviour using a think-aloud technique.

RECORD OF READING BEHAVIOUR

Name: Susan		Title: Colours	
Age:		Series: Mac Millan	Seen
Date: 5/ 6 /93		Stage: 1:2	(Unseen)

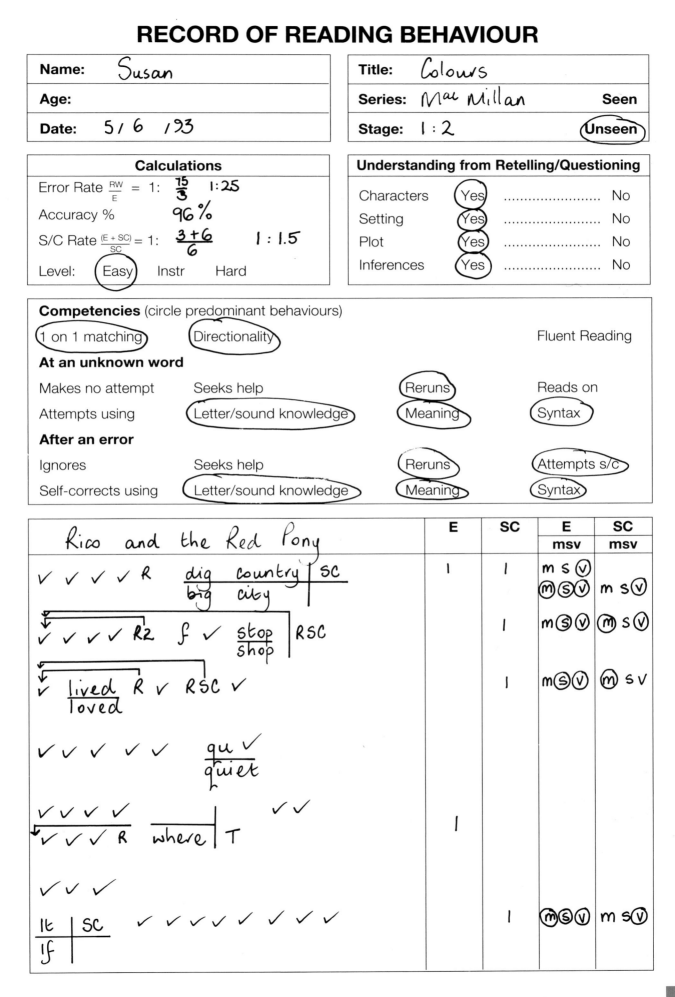

Calculations	Understanding from Retelling/Questioning

Calculations

Error Rate $\frac{RW}{E}$ = 1: $\frac{75}{3}$ 1:25

Accuracy %   96%

S/C Rate $\frac{(E + SC)}{SC}$ = 1: $\frac{3+6}{6}$ 1 : 1.5

Level: (Easy)   Instr   Hard

Understanding from Retelling/Questioning

Characters	(Yes)	....	No
Setting	(Yes)	....	No
Plot	(Yes)	....	No
Inferences	(Yes)	....	No

Competencies (circle predominant behaviours)

(1 on 1 matching)   (Directionality)   Fluent Reading

At an unknown word

Makes no attempt	Seeks help	(Reruns)	Reads on
Attempts using	(Letter/sound knowledge)	(Meaning)	(Syntax)

After an error

Ignores	Seeks help	(Reruns)	(Attempts s/c)
Self-corrects using	(Letter/sound knowledge)	(Meaning)	(Syntax)

	E	SC	E msv	SC msv
Rico and the Red Pony				
✓ ✓ ✓ ✓ R $\frac{dig}{big}$ $\frac{country}{city}$ | SC	1	1	m s (v) / (m)(s)(v)	m s (v)
✓ ✓ ✓ ✓ R2 ʃ ✓ $\frac{stop}{shop}$ | RSC		1	m (s)(v)	(m) s (v)
✓ $\frac{lived}{loved}$ R ✓ RSC ✓		1	m (s)(v)	(m) s v
✓ ✓ ✓ ✓ ✓ $\frac{qu ✓}{quiet}$				
✓ ✓ ✓ ✓ ✓✓ ✓ ✓ ✓ R where | T	1			
✓ ✓ ✓				
$\frac{It}{If}$ | SC ✓ ✓ ✓ ✓ ✓ ✓ ✓		1	(m)(s)(v)	m s(v)

	E	SC	E msv	SC msv
✓ way/why ✓ RSC ✓ ✓		1	m s Ⓥ	Ⓜ Ⓢ v
✓ ✓ ✓ ✓ ✓				
✓ ✓ did/don't ✓ ✓	1		m Ⓢ v	
way/why	sc ✓ ✓ mm/move ✓ ✓		1	m s Ⓥ	Ⓜ Ⓢ v
✓ ✓ did ✓/didn't ✓ ✓ ✓ ✓				
	3	6		
TOTAL				

Susan had not seen the story before and although her teacher had introduced it to her, her reading was very stilted. At unknown words, Susan reran the sentence, phrase, or word in order to gather up the meaning, and used this with her knowledge of language and letter sound relationships to predict what might come next. After errors, she attempted to correct her reading herself. Her retelling showed an understanding of characters, setting, plot, and inferences. Her accuracy was 96%.

Susan needs a program that equips her with strategies that promote and maintain fluency so that, using her prior knowledge, her oral language, and her knowledge of print, she can process the text more quickly. Her teacher's prompts will be towards reading more like she talks. Her teacher will ensure that Susan gets lots of fluent reading practice on familiar material and, if necessary, will model the behaviour required to make it explicit.

Establishing a baseline

In order to establish a baseline, it is important to take a record of each child's reading behaviour during the first four to six weeks of the year. Most children in their first year at school will not be ready to read published texts at this time. We would suggest that you ask the child to draw you a picture and tell you a story about it. A one- or two-line story at the most is appropriate. You record the story for the child, reading it as you write. When you have finished, ask the child to read the story back to you using his or her finger. Check, score, and analyse the story using the usual conventions.

Ongoing monitoring and evaluation

You should continue to monitor your children's reading behaviour by taking records at least once a month and at other important times, such as:

- when you think the children are ready to progress to more challenging reading material;
- when there is a significant unexplained change in reading behaviour;
- before reporting to parents.

Each time, you should make comparisons with the previous record to find out if the children have:

- ❏ acquired and demonstrated understanding of content;
- ❏ applied strategies;
- ❏ demonstrated the acquisition of skills;
- ❏ made progress.

You can use these Records of Reading Behaviour in conjunction with your formal and informal writing checks and your incidental observations to help you design your instructional program and form *ad hoc* groups for particular instruction.

Incidental observations

By watching children informally and making anecdotal notes, you can learn much about children's attitudes, interests, and expertise in reading, including the type of materials, topics, and genres they choose to read and write about. Many important, culturally different, home literacy practises that are not apparent in a more formal setting may surface during this informal time. A useful way to do this is to take time to note and record what children do when:

- a choice of reading activities is offered;
- participating in a class or group Language Experience or Shared Reading lessons;

- reading independently;
- talking about books they have read;
- writing;
- involved in self-directed learning activities at learning centres.

Collecting samples of children's work

Collecting samples of children's work can also give valuable insight into reading strategies and comprehension. Samples of children's writing can show strengths that are also applicable to reading, for example, directionality, one-to-one matching, the ability to make connections between sounds and letters, and the ability to reread their own written language.

Many teachers are concerned about some children's understanding of the material they are reading. In order to monitor comprehension when you are not working individually, you could ask the children to complete some of the activities described in Chapter 7. These samples can be added to the child's assessment portfolio.

Many of the responses to text are related directly to the child's understanding of the story. For example:

Understanding the entire story
- ❏ Can the child retell and/or respond to the story in oral, written, and visual language?

Understanding characters and relationships
- ❏ Can the child describe orally, in writing, and/or by drawing the main character, important characters, or favourite character?
- ❏ Can the child make a web showing the characters or showing the relationship between the characters?

Understanding the plot
- ❏ Can the child draw pictures to show the sequence of the story, or make a time line for the story, or match pictures with sentences describing the events in the story?
- ❏ Can the child put the sentences in order?

Understanding the setting
- ❏ Can the child draw a map of where the story took place?
- ❏ Can they make a map of all the places visited by the characters in the story

A checklist of early reading behaviours and a
sample Record of Reading Behaviour are included
in the Appendix to assist you with monitoring.

9 Writing

Children who write every day learn that speaking, writing, and reading are all interrelated parts of language. They learn that most of the words they encounter when reading are the same ones as they use in their own speech and writing. When children write something meaningful to them, they gain specific understandings about the structure of their language and more easily grasp other people's ideas when reading. These understandings can be further reinforced if children are given many opportunities for both accessing and expressing information using other modes of language in a balanced literacy program.

Knowledge of the conventions of writing can occur incidentally without the child being aware of what is happening, vicariously when he watches what someone else does, and collaboratively because someone else helps him to express what he wants to say in writing.

In your classroom, your role is to encourage children to write and to demonstrate how to choose a topic or write in a particular genre, and to revise and edit, in mini-lessons or conferences throughout the year. In this way, you help your students to acquire the strategies they need to become competent writers. They can also begin to understand that writers approach their tasks in different ways. These writing strategies are outlined in Chapter 2, "A Balanced Language Program." Some writers like to work in a very organised way but not all writers brainstorm or make topic lists before they start writing. We must allow children to find and develop their own preferred system.

Young writers often find the notion of redrafting a piece of their writing tedious and daunting. In such cases, you can scaffold the task by taking over the actual rewriting while asking the child what he or she wants to say and allowing them to see how we go about "fixing up" anything we have written. This joint reconstruction of the child's work is a real learning experience for them if the conference is handled sensitively. Another way to help is for you to put the first draft on a computer and to work with the child as they edit their work. It is then a simple matter for the final draft to be printed out.

It is more important that children learn how to edit

their own writing rather than spending valuable time rewriting.

Many children will already be well on the way to having control over some conventions of writing before they start school as a result of their interactions with their environments, e.g., road signs, advertisements, TV, board games, and books. They continue this learning at school in print-saturated classrooms where, every day, teachers and children read and write about things that interest them, together and independently. In such an environment, children soon come to understand that:

- Written text needs to make sense.
- Letters make up words, and words combine to make sentences.
- Each spoken word corresponds with a written word.
- There are differing patterns of speech and writing.
- The symbols they encounter in print are associated with sounds.
- Print moves from left to right with return sweep; one spoken word mapping on to one written word.
- The conventions of print are consistent.
- Spelling has consistencies and irregularities.
- The spellings of new words are sometimes similar to the spellings of some familiar ones, and some words have more than one spelling.
- Some words have more than one meaning and several words can have similar meanings.
- Focusing on a word when it is being written helps to recognise it later.
- They can write about some of the same things that happen in the books they read.

Support for beginning writers

In the first years of school, your main teaching task will be to help children to:

- articulate their thoughts;
- gain alphabet name knowledge;
- gain sound letter associations;
- build a bank of known words;
- make analogies;
- use what they know to help them get to what they don't know.

As well as this important teaching, your role in the writing focus of your literacy program is to:

- Build on the literacy competencies that children bring with them to school.
- Recognise and value each child's cultural background, experiences, language, and contribution. Mutual trust is an important ingredient in the teacher/child partnership.
- Provide a stimulating, print-saturated environment with access to a wide variety of reading and writing materials: different authors, genres and themes, different coloured, shaped, and sized paper, and a variety of pencils and coloured pens.
- Provide for independent reading and writing every day. During this time, children can be encouraged to use the strategies that have been part of your instructional program. For instance, they can be guided to ask themselves these kinds of questions when they are uncertain how to spell a word.

"Shall I make a link with another word that sounds/looks like this one?"
"Shall I sound the word out?"
"Do I know this word already?"
"Have I got it in another story?"
"Is it somewhere else in the room?"
"Is it in my personal list?"
"If I reread the sentence so far, will that help me?"

This integration of strategies is of prime importance. Provide an oral language time daily, especially for those children who enter school speaking less fluently than others in their class. Initiate a one-to-one conversation with each child in the class every day. The approach to writing outlined later in this chapter enables you to engage in this vital dialogue with children from their very first day at school. You will often find that children will share ideas individually that they have not volunteered in a group situation, and a very warm and caring partnership can be built between you. The child realises that what he has to say is valued by you because you give him your whole attention when he is speaking. This also gives you the opportunity to encourage the child to talk more by asking such questions as:

"**What** happened next?"
"**How** did you feel then?"
"**Why** do you think they did that?"
"**Which** one is your favourite?"

"**What** did your family think of that?"
"**Where** were you going in the car?"

You should regularly be using other strategies to help your children:

- Act as a scribe to interpret a child's thoughts when and if needed. The use of the child's own language is vital.
- Read aloud to the children each day to familiarise them with the language patterns and vocabulary used in books. Use some of these excerpts as models for writing.
- Model uses for writing and provide daily demonstrations accompanied by "thinking aloud" so children have insight into the process as well as the product. Children need to see that language is a way of representing experiences and that written language can be a product of their own experiences. You can do this by writing about your own experiences, making lists, composing letters, etc., in front of the class.

Some teachers demonstrate how an expert writes by modelling purposes of writing for their class each day. To begin with, you can record simple statements about the day of the week, the weather, etc., for your emergent writers on a chart in the following way.

Teacher: Can anyone tell me what day it is today?
Child: It's Tuesday.
Teacher: Yes, it is Tuesday today. I'll write that on our news chart. I'll start by writing "today".
(The following questions help to develop directionality)
Where will I start writing? Who can come and show me on the chart?
(Child points to right-hand side of the page)
That was a good try.
(Takes child's hand and guides it to the left-hand edge of the paper.)
This is where we begin. What letter does "today" begin with?
Child: A "t", like Tommy's name.
Teacher: Yes, it does start with a "t". I'll use a capital letter because it's the beginning of my sentence. Watch while I write "Today".
(Writes while saying the word aloud slowly.)
Now I'll leave a space before I write the next word "is".
(Writes "is".)

Now I will write "Tuesday". Can anyone tell me what letter "Tuesday" starts with?

Child: A "t", like "today".

Teacher: Yes, it is a "T" and it will have to be another capital letter "T" because it's the name of the day. Watch while I write "Tuesday" and listen as I say the word. *(Writes "Tuesday".)*
That's the end of that sentence. Does anyone know what we need to put at the end of a sentence?

Child: A question mark?

Teacher: Sometimes we have to put a question mark. That's when we are asking a question. At the end of a sentence we put a full stop like this. *(Places full stop in appropriate place.)*
Now let's read this together to check and see if our sentence says what we want it to.
(Points to words as children read.)

Continue to reinforce directionality, spacing, and return sweep until this session is complete. Some other teaching points could be taken but only if they are appropriate to the needs of your children and for only a short period of time.

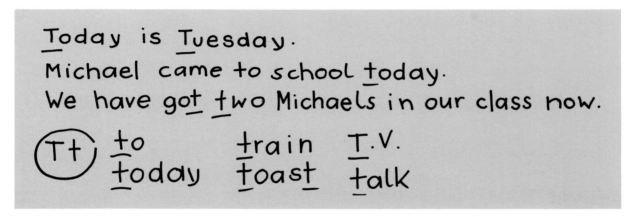

For more advanced writers you could involve the children even more in the process by asking children to help you write letters and words in sentences on the chart. This is a good time to do some word analysis as well. The children can also assist with punctuation. This is an ideal opportunity to demonstrate the use of speech marks, full stops, commas, question marks, and exclamation marks. You can also extend and enrich vocabulary by trying out different words and phrases until you are satisfied with the result.

Another way to include your pupils in the writing demonstration is to choose a child who has an interesting experience to recount to assist you in the oral discussion leading up to recording. You will be demonstrating how to organise your thoughts to make a coherent, interesting account of an event told by someone else. The child can begin by telling the group about an event and then encouraging others to ask questions. If children select a card with a question starter word on it, this will help them to compose their questions. Suitable words are:

What?	Where?	When?	Why?
How?	Did?	Do?	Are?
Could?	Were?	Was?	Will?

Table 14   Modelling Aspects of the Writing Process

NEWS DISCUSSION	TEACHER'S SUMMARY OF DISCUSSION WRITTEN IN THIRD PERSON DURING THE DIALOGUE.
Teacher: You had a very interesting piece of news today Lucy. Could you come and tell me about it please? (Teacher records the date and her comments on a chart in front of the class.	It is Friday 29th March today. Lucy has some interesting news for us today.
Lucy: My Dad took me to the motor car racing on Saturday and it was very exciting. Would anyone like to ask me a question? Yes, Jarrod.	Her father took her to the motor car racing on Saturday and she said it was very exciting.
Jarrod: (Selects a card with *Why* on it and asks a question.) Why did you think it was exciting?	
Lucy: Six cars crashed in a big pile up on a slippery bend.	Six cars crashed in a big pile up on a slippery bend.
Sally: (Selects a card with *What* on it and asks a question.) What made the cars crash?	A wheel came off one of the cars and that made it skid in front of the other cars.
Eric: (Selects a card with *Was* on it and asks a question.) Was anyone hurt?	Luckily only one driver had to go in the ambulance to hospital. He had a broken leg.
Karen: (Selects a card with *Do* on it and asks a question.) Do you want to go to the motor racing again?	
Lucy: I can't wait to go to the motor racing again. Teacher: I'll report the last part of Lucy's story like this.	Lucy can't wait to go to the motor racing again.

During this interchange, the teacher recorded
Lucy's story on a chart.

It is Friday, 29th March today.
Lucy has some interesting news for us today.
Her father took her to the motor car racing
on Saturday and she said it was very exciting.
Six cars crashed in a big pile up on a slippery bend.
A wheel came off one of the cars
and that made it skid in front of the other cars.
Luckily, only one driver had to go in the
ambulance to hospital. He had a broken leg.
Lucy can't wait to go to the motor racing again.

Help children to use writing themselves by scaffolding the task as necessary. For example, to help children acquire the sound letter associations of the alphabet you may provide each child with a small alphabet picture card to assist them to make links using familiar pictures while writing. You may also make links between letters/sounds and words which have been encountered in familiar books. To help with the acquisition of new written vocabulary, you can encourage the children to build up their own personal bank of words that are important to them. These words can be written on cards and given to them for learning and subsequently be written in personal dictionaries.

How Maui slowed the Sun

Maui and his brothers
PB b B bp   MEⒸHLA

Maui slowed the sun.
PBtotoF obF oЄo

The sun was too fast.
w Ubbpwb gore

The sun   was   asleep.
the d nwescep

                    and
to sa qⒽDM

Maui   catched   it   too.
MpuiCADito

The above example shows how the teacher scaffolded the task for Meohla during a "drop-in" conference. Meohla had been working independently on her story of how Maui slowed the sun while the teacher had been helping other children. Meohla had been using the upper- and lower-case letters she knew well to represent her story. When the teacher dropped in on Meohla, she was able to remind her that there were some words that she wanted in her story that she could already write, and some that were in the room for her to copy. She also reminded her that she should say the word she wanted slowly to herself and write down the letters she could hear. The teacher waited until Meohla had written "the" and started "sun" and then left to work with another child. The remainder of Meohla's story shows that she used the knowledge that the teacher reminded her that she had.

The ways that you can help children grasp the writing process come in many forms. Always try to enrich language and encourage creativity.

Encourage children to use the environment to find words they need in their stories. This may include asking another child, going on a print walk each day, looking in a poem, song, or previous story, or looking in the dictionary.

Share a variety of poems, songs, language chants, and plays that incorporate rhyme and alliteration.

Provide an alphabet centre with many activities for reinforcing alphabet letter names and corresponding sounds. This area should include plastic magnetic letters for children to experiment with word and sentence building activities, e.g., use four letters to make a word, change one letter to make another word, make today's weather sentence with the magnetic letters.

Help children to learn how to proofread and edit their own writing. Many young children forget what was written on the previous day and it is preferable to edit their writing with them "on the run" and not wait until they have finished. Editing can be difficult for them to achieve successfully on their own and they will need plenty of support while they are learning this skill.

There are two schools of thought regarding the

71

editing process. One suggests that your aim is to have children integrate all the writing strategies. This would lead to children editing as they write, leaving only minor changes to be made before publication. The other point of view suggests that children need to get their thoughts on paper and not worry about the surface features of writing as these can be fixed later. Whichever opinion you subscribe to, it is necessary for you to encourage children to reread their stories both as they write, and when they have finished writing them.

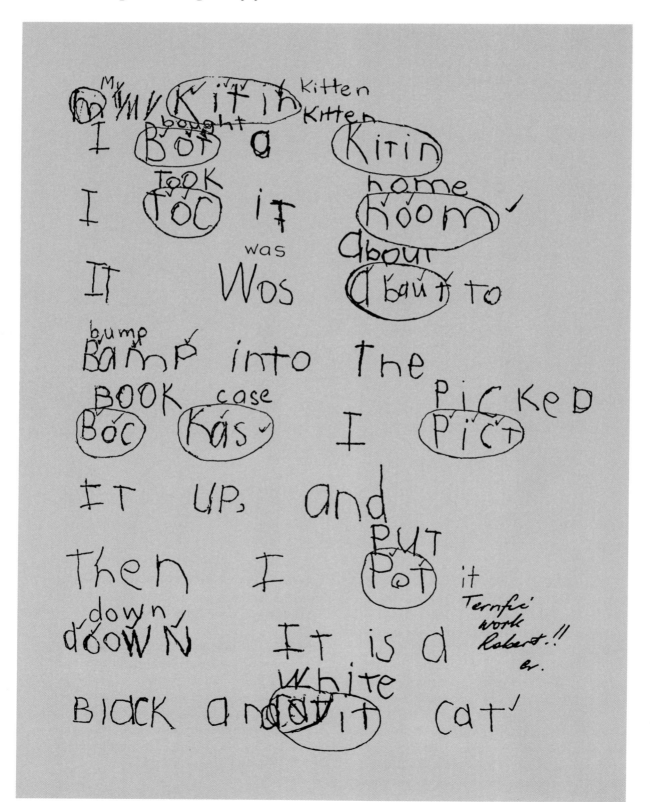

Because Robert's teacher knows that he is able to work independently, she encourages him to write as much as he can, circling the words he thinks are not spelled correctly as he goes. When he has finished writing, he is required to check in his personal spelling book, the dictionary if he is able to use one, to search around the room, and to correct as many words as he can before he meets with the teacher for a conference.

Discuss ways that your class can find words they need independently by asking someone else in the class, using words in their environment, or looking in a dictionary

Encourage the children to build up their own personal "bank" of words that are important to them. These words can be written on cards and given to them. They can become part of their writing vocabulary by making and unmaking these words with plastic magnetic letters and then writing the words in their personal dictionaries.

Writing Purposes and Forms

To provide a balanced writing focus in your classroom, you need to engage the children in a wide range of forms and purposes of written language. These will be decided by the learning objectives you have in mind and the requirements of the curriculum.

These experiences will eventually lead to the children being able to organise the written language in their environment in the same way that they arrange the rest of their experiences.

They will be able to communicate with others and express their feelings through writing, organise information, categorise elements, and put information in numerical and/or alphabetical order. They will learn how to:

- Record their feelings and observations in personal letters, reports on science experiments, narrative writing, poetry, diaries, journals, and observations of the world around them.

M uscle shells clinging
U nderwater volcano
R ushing waters
I ron sand
W aves smashing on the rocks
A nemones sucking fingers
I nteresting sea squirts

- Retell a favourite story in their own words.

Sam

The monsters were having a party in the closet.

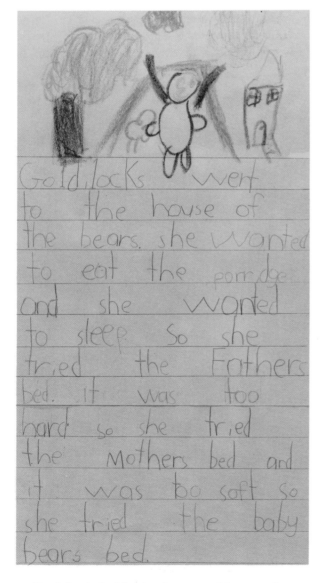

Goldilocks went to the house of the bears. she wanted to eat the porridge and she wanted to sleep so she tried the Fathers bed. it was too hard so she tried the Mothers bed and it was too soft so she tried the baby bears bed.

- Explain their thinking in note-taking, rough notes, interpretation of maps, graphs, diagrams, etc.

Facts I know about spiders now

When you touch a spider it feels all funny.

The orbweb spider is scared of water.

When a redback spider bites you on the leg you can die or you could get very sick.

Spiders make their webs to catch their prey.

SPIDERS

Daddy Long Legs has six legs

Spiders have eight legs.

The redback spiders are very dangerous.

- Describe a sequence of events, a friend or a character in a book, advertisements, labels, and signs.

LIFE BEING A GANNET
I saw a silver flash, so I dived into the sea.
I missed so I dived again.
I caught this fish for once and for all.
I swallowed the fish.
Then when I got back I regurgitated my fish.
I gave it to my babies.
I said, "I hope it's good."
I flew away and I landed on a rock.
The rock was sandy.
I snuggled down into the sand.
After that I fell asleep.
I woke up an hour later.
I felt hungry so I went down to catch a fish.
I caught sight of a silver flash.
I dived into the sea and I caught my fish.
I went back to my babies and regurgitated my fish.
When I go over the sea I glide.
I glide softly like a cloud.
I soar across the sky like a balloon that's been let go.
When I come in to land I have to wait,
Because I need the right temperature of wind.

- Inform others about future events in a poster, news scripts, meeting minutes and agenda, invitations, and schedules.

When the firemen go to a fire They use. the hose. They Wear their helmets So They don't get Wet and When They Come back They have tea. Meredith

- Influence others through advertisements and commercials, letters to members of parliament and newspaper editors, discussion notes, and cartoons.
- Communicate with others through letters, requests for information, question surveys, and greeting cards.
- Form predictions or hypotheses about possible outcomes in stories, and in health, art, science, and social studies.
- Compare and contrast information in charts, diagrams, graphs, and descriptions.

Make a graph which shows how many of each of these are on the island : Motels — Hospitals—Shops.

Motels	Hospitals	Shops
X		
X		X
X		X
X	X	X
X	X	X

There are more motels than hospitals
There are 5 motels and 2 hospitals.
5 > 2 The difference is 3.

I have 4 shops.
There are more shops than hospitals. The difference is 2.

- Give directions for others to follow a recipe, the rules for playing a game, stage directions for a play, health and safety rules, and the sequence for making a kite, etc.

Monitoring Children's Writing

How will you know if your pupils are making progress?

There are different ways of monitoring writing progress: some periodic, some on-going, some formal, and some informal. We recommend that you use a combination of these in order to get a true picture of both what a child can do at a particular point in time, and what a child has learned to do over a period of time. If you use a variety of records, especially those which are ongoing and observational, to help you determine the strengths and needs of the children in your class, you will find that you quickly come to know more about your children and are in a strong position to make powerful educational decisions.

Formal in-class checks

We suggest that in the first four to six weeks of the school year you make a formal in-class check. In the first year we would recommend a check that includes oral language, letter identification, and writing. A sample of such a check, and instructions for its administration, is included in the Appendix. An early writing behaviour checklist for use at other times is also included. At the beginning of year two, we would recommend using the writing task and the dictation task from the Observation Survey (Clay, 1993).

At the beginning of year three, we would recommend a simple spelling test and a teacher-directed written sample.

You can use these beginning of year checks to help you to design your instructional program and form *ad hoc* groups for particular instruction. Formal in-class checks later in the year can help you to assess whether your instruction has been appropriate to the needs of the children. You may ask yourself if the children have:

❑ acquired and demonstrated understanding of the content?
❑ applied the strategies?
❑ demonstrated the acquisition of skills?
❑ made progress?

Writing samples

In conjunction with periodic formal checks, we also recommend the collecting of writing samples at regular intervals during the school year. The regular collection of writing samples can help you to:

- Maintain a balanced writing program. If the samples you collect are all from the same register, it may be that you are over-emphasising this aspect or neglecting others. Likewise, if samples in one area appear to be producing better results than those in another area, it may again be a reflection of your emphasis.
- Group children with similar needs into groups for instructional purposes. These groups may reflect, for example, those children who need extra assistance with some part of the spelling process or those children who need extra help with the generation and recording of ideas. These groups will be flexible and meet together only if and when necessary.
- Keep track of individual progress. If you collect writing samples at regular intervals throughout the year, you will have evidence of how a child is gaining control over the conventions of writing over time, rather than just the writing product at any one point in time.
- Observe particular strengths/weaknesses in individual children's writing ability.

Some of the questions you may ask yourself as you read a child's writing sample are:

❑ Is the child using a variety of methods to solve unknown words in spelling?
❑ Does this child know how to write an ever increasing number of short, high frequency words correctly without help?
❑ Does this child know how to hear and record the sounds in words in sequence?

    unkl   mawntin

❑ Do some of this child's spelling attempts have visual similarity?

    becasue   lttlie
    because   little

❑ Does this child know how to move flexibly within words by making links from the known to the unknown? Can the child add frequently used endings, e.g., look, looks, looked, looking? Can the child substitute initial letters/letter clusters, e.g., pot, lot, got, hot, slot, trot? Can the child add different initial letters/letter clusters, e.g., and, sand, hand, band, brand, strand? Can the child substitute final letters/letter clusters, e.g., car, cat, can, cart? Can the child substitute medial letters, e.g., pit, pat, pot, put, pout?

❑ Is this child starting to use some common spelling patterns, e.g., boat, coat, float, running, skipping, making, coming?

❑ Is there evidence that the child is starting to use print resources in the room, e.g., using familiar books, poems, charts, wall stories, and a dictionary?

❑ Is there evidence of appropriate use of print conventions, e.g., spatial concepts, such as left-to-right spacing between words and return sweeps; correct letter formation, speed,

legibility, beauty of form, appropriate use of upper- and lower-case letters; punctuation, use of conventions, sentences, and paragraphs?

❑ Is this child able to generate quality ideas and language?

❑ Is this child able to sustain /develop ideas and language across several sentences and paragraphs?

❑ Is the child's writing a suitable length for its purpose?

❑ Is this child developing the skills of proofreading and editing?

❑ What are the next most important strategies for this child to control?

Analysing Writing Samples

Michelle aged 6.7

This is the caravan place and you could go to the caravan place if you might want to go to the caravan place you could bye a caravan if you want to go to the caravan place you can play in the caravan it is a nice day to go to a caravan place.

Analysis

Michelle's strength lies in her ability to record a number of words, correctly using words that are already part of her writing vocabulary, and words that she has accessed from other print resources in the room. She needs assistance with punctuation, and in expressing her ideas so that they are more interesting to the reader.

Teaching strategies

A group of children who had similar needs to

Michelle were drawn together. Michelle agreed that her story could be made into an overhead projector transparency so that all the children could read it and suggest how it might be made more interesting. They started by suggesting other words that Michelle could have used instead of *place*. They suggested *park* and *camping ground*. Next, they saw the need to describe the park or camping ground so that the reader would know what it looked like. They worked co-operatively giving Michelle ideas that the teacher recorded on another overhead transparency. Finally they suggested how the remainder of the story might be condensed. Each child then returned to work individually on his or her own story using the procedures that the group had suggested.

B.J. aged 6.11

My Dad Took me
in The fielde!
be BJ

Oen Day my Dad
dint no Ther wer
skunks and snaks
in The Fieald and
he Touk me in the
fieald.

but I The Skunk
Stikt his Tel up in
The der up my
nose and I sniff
it up and it Stunk
so bad I skremd

I ran in The
kichun and Tuke
ten cans of
Tmadochoos!

and it bint wruk
so I ran in the
bathroom and
Took a shawr
Ti Workte

Analysis

B.J.'s strength lies in his ability to express himself in an interesting way. Although he is able to spell many high frequency words correctly, he still relies heavily on a combination of visual memory and hearing and recording the sounds for most of his spelling. This often leads to unnecessary inaccuracies. He needs to add more words to his bank of known words and also needs to have an appreciation of when words don't "look right", so that he is able to initiate some checking.

Teaching strategies

B.J. and his teacher worked together in an individual conference situation. The teacher started by expressing her delight with B.J.'s story, and asking him if he could tell her why it was the best he had ever written. He was unable to, so she explained that it was really interesting, that she could see in her mind's eye where he had been, and that he had said it in an artistic way. She also gave credit for the words that he was able to spell correctly, and then asked what he felt it needed before it could be published. He knew some of the spelling was incorrect. He agreed with the teacher that there were some words in the story it would be good for him to be able to spell correctly as he would use them again. To this end he agreed to learn to spell—*one, there, were, took, didn't, tail*—and wrote them in his personal spelling book. He could ask the teacher to test him on these words later in the week when he felt he had mastered them. The teacher then pointed out the mismatch between the sound and spelling of touk, tuke, (took) that he was to learn and made a link from that word to "look" and "book" which he already knew. She then made both visual and aural links to other words ending in the same way. The remaining spelling errors she corrected for him by saying and writing other words in the same way, e.g.,

cook   hook   tail   wail   sail   bail   fail

She showed him the "ed" ending on screamed (skremd) and sniffed (snift). The remaining spelling errors she corrected for him.

When the teachers of both Michelle and B. J. collect their next writing samples, they will be looking for evidence that the teaching points they have made are reflected in the work. To this end, both teachers made brief notes that they attached to the writing sample.

Reluctant Writers

In print-rich classrooms where children are required to write daily, many children quickly learn how to translate their thoughts into a written form that can be easily read by their classmates. However, there are some children who for one reason or another, find it hard to get underway with writing. Such a child is Philip.

Philip aged 7.6

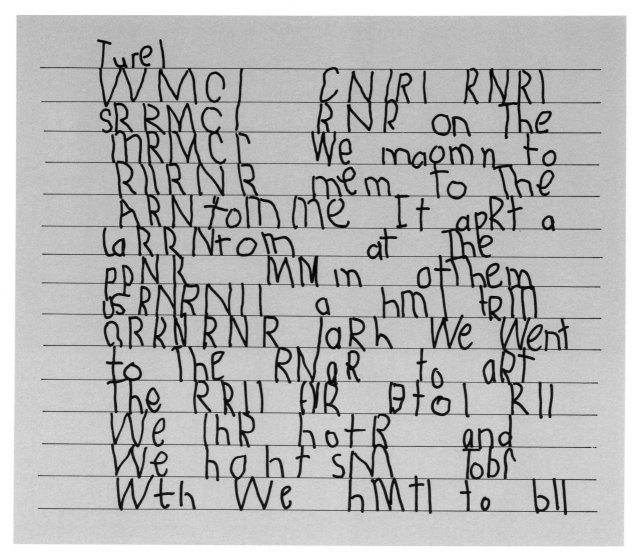

Translation

My dad cut his finger on the machine. We had to take him to the hospital. It took a long time at the hospital. Mum got us a hot chocolate drink. Then we went to the chemist to get pills for Dad. We went home and then we had some tea. Then we went to bed.

Analysis

Philip does not like writing because he has realised that his output does not resemble the work achieved by others in the class. He has a small bank of words that he knows how to write but he is often unable to read what he has written. He has many sound/letter confusions and his attempts to spell words indicate that there are inconsistencies in his confusions, e.g., "DNIRI/Dtol" for "Dad" and "maomn/hoht" for "had". He uses a mixture of upper and lower case letters, usually inappropriately. Philip had difficulty in reading his work after it was written but he was able to match one spoken word with each invented spelling of a word on the page.

Teaching strategies

Philip's teacher recognised that his failure to develop sufficient attention to the details of print had prevented him from acquiring the skill required to construct a working writing vocabulary. She worked with him in an individual conference situation daily because of his need to have her supportive guidance during the exploration process to help him overcome his confusions. Philip told her that he didn't enjoy writing, saying that he "wasn't any good at writing". He accepted her offer of help with enthusiasm and the provision of an alphabet card to help him to sort out his letter/sound confusions as he was writing helped him to acquire confidence and skill in this area. She also encouraged him to build up a bank of high frequency words so that he didn't have to labour over every word as he was writing.

For children such as Philip the following teaching steps have been found to be very effective:

Teaching steps for children having difficulties

It is important to note that children do not move through writing steps in a linear way nor do they necessarily follow the same steps as other children. Each child is unique, and your careful observations of writing behaviour will help you tailor your program to suit each child's individual needs.

Step 1

Try a dictated caption, written by you, and read by the child. It is important that the child observes closely as you write and listens as you explain what you are doing. In this way you are making explicit the strategies you are using to advance composition in writing and comprehension in reading. Watching you, the "expert" at work, enables the child to see how you generate and develop ideas in writing and his needs are met in a supportive, guided situation.

Julie

I saw a big crayfish

under the water and

it was shaking.

You were lucky to see a big crayfish.

At the completion of the writing the child is asked to read back what you have written. This immediate reading back is vital as you can guide the reinforcement of emergent reading procedures.

Step 2

The child is encouraged to transfer knowledge about sounds and letters. To facilitate the child's developing letter sound knowledge, it is helpful to

have an alphabet card in front of you.

Teacher:	What are you going to write about today?
Child:	(No response)
Teacher:	Would you like to write about the picture you have drawn? *(Make only one suggestion at a time.)*
Child:	I want to write about my house.
Teacher:	What are you going to say?

Child:	My house is waiting for a family.
Teacher:	That's an interesting way to start. Where will we begin on the page? **(Some children may need help with this. A spot in the correct place helps as a guide.)**
Child:	(Points to top left of page.)
Teacher:	Can you write "My"?
Child:	No.
Teacher:	What can you hear in "My"?
Child:	I can hear an "M" but I can't remember what it looks like.
Teacher:	Yes, it does have an "M" in it. You could look on your alphabet card and find it.
Child:	Here it is.
Teacher:	Will it be a capital "M" or a little letter "m"?
Child:	A capital?
Teacher:	Yes! Why do you use a capital?
Child:	Because it's the start of my story?
Teacher:	Yes, you found out about that yesterday.
Child:	(Writes capital "M" in the correct place.)
Teacher:	Here is the other letter in "my"… *(Writes "y".)* Now we have written "my". Can you write "house"?
Child:	No.
Teacher:	Can you hear anything in "house"? Say it slowly and listen carefully, "h-o-u-s-e". *(Do not isolate the sounds.)*
Child:	A "c"?
Teacher:	That was a good try. It's an "s". We'll write the word. Can you show me where to write it?

Child:	There. *(Indicates that a space needs to be left.)*
Teacher:	Good. *(Writes "house" pointing out where the "s" goes in the word and encouraging the child to write "s" in the appropriate place.)* Can you write "is"?
Child:	I know how to write that word. *(Realises there is no room left on the line and begins to write on next line at left end of page.)*
Teacher:	You knew where to next on the page. That's great. What can you hear in "waiting"?
Child:	(No response.)
Teacher:	Where will we write it?
Child:	(Child points.)
Teacher:	Yes, that's the place. *(Writes "waiting".)* Now, what can you hear in "for"?
Child:	"f". *(Writes "f".)*
Teacher:	*(Completes word.)* Can you write the word "a"?
Child:	No.
Teacher:	*(Writes word and when child makes no response writes "family" too.)* What goes at the end of a sentence?
Child:	A full stop. *(Puts it at the end of the story.)*
Teacher:	You know a lot about writing, don't you. I'd like to hear you read your story now. We can see if it makes sense and if we need to make any changes.

My house is waiting for a family. Charlotte.

This reading of the completed story is vital as it reinforces early reading strategies.

The child can read it with the teacher, to a friend, or to his or her family.

During the above procedure it is unnecessary to labour over encouraging the child to hear sounds in words. Stretching the words once or twice is sufficient. It is very important not to isolate sounds in words. It is also important that the child watches while the teacher writes and is involved in the process.

At this point the teacher could suggest that the child might choose a word from their story to add to their personal bank of "words I know how to write". New words can be added to their personal dictionary or to a concertina-type dictionary. The plastic letters mentioned earlier can be used to practise making the word, e.g., "my" from the story just written.

If the teacher is busy and the child wants to write a longer story than the teacher has time for, she either scribes the rest of the story for the child, or suggests that the child attempts the rest by himself.

Richard

I got my presents. I got a bulldozer and wedding shoes and a wedding suit for when Mum gets married.

Step 3

When the children are attempting more difficult words a trialling or "try card" is introduced. This can be a portion of the page that he is working on. You should encourage the child to check his attempts by making links with other known words and looking for it in another story or around the room before seeking help form you. A tick (check) to indicate letters and/or words correctly identified gives positive encouragement to the child and helps him recognise what he knows. This "trying out" of words before checking the attempt encourages the child to use reasoning as an important factor in the process of learning to spell and it also develops an independent learning attitude.

The bear and the man went looking for treasure in the forest and they found gold. The forest was dark and they heard an owl hooting. ☺

Were they frightened when they heard the owl hooting? I enjoyed your story. Kylie

trăsha
treasure

fŏrĭsf
forest

fŏwd
found

gŏled
gold

hŏtĭng
hooting

ŏwl
owl

wăs
was

dăk
dark

hĕrd
heard

When the child has several basic words he can write, he is encouraged to write independently. Many children at this point are able to write their stories without checking their spelling of words until they have finished. This can be done during a conference with you.

Other children like to continue to use a "try" card on which they attempt the spelling of new or unfamiliar words. These are then checked with you, a parent, helper, a peer tutor, or a dictionary. Praise is given for any attempts made and the correct model is provided underneath.

e.g.   <u>throte</u>   <u>becos</u>
       throat   because

Teacher: *(Writes the correct version.)*
Did you get the "thr" in throat because you knew another word that started like that?

Child: Yes. "Three" starts the same way.
Teacher: You nearly got the whole word. Some of the words which have an "o" sound do end in "ote" but this one ends with "oat" like "boat".
(In this way the children get a visual and aural example.)

This example of scaffolded instruction illustrates how a child can advance under the guidance of a more competent tutor and is helped to make links from the known to the unknown. In time, the child will be able to control the task himself and thus he has acquired a new skill. Until that happens, the tutor is scaffolding the learning task to enable the child to perform a task he would otherwise be unable to attempt.

In this approach, children frequently check their writing by rereading what they have written to see if it makes sense and often consult other children or the teacher about it. These consultations provide for the one-to-one interaction so strongly recommended by recent research.

The main ideas underlining this approach to writing are that it is the unique and personal interaction between you and the child at crucial points of understanding and comprehension that assist the learning of the complex spelling, reading, and writing patterns of our language. Many children can and do make the transition from approximated to standard spelling and writing procedures easily and naturally by making their own active comparisons—but this is not so for all children. These children need sensitive monitoring, and will benefit from support and explicit instruction on some occasions. The writing process outlined here is based on the conviction that when children actively take part in meaningful reading and writing experiences, they come to understand that each process substantially aids the other and that they can control them both.

10 Oral Language

The importance of the interactive nature of reading, writing, and oral language cannot be overstressed in the early years of literacy acquisition. The more children read and are read to, the more words, concepts, and language patterns become part of their listening vocabulary. Soon children are using these words in their everyday oral language and including them in their writing. The more sophisticated their oral language becomes, the more understandings and vocabulary they have to bring to the tasks of reading and writing.

The reality of today's classroom is that many children entering school come with a language or language dialect different from that of the teacher. It is your task, while accepting and valuing these differences, to ensure that children become effective communicators and active listeners. It is not the intention of this chapter to debate whether children speaking English as a second or third language should be taught to read and write in their mother tongue. Our aim is to help you to help the children in your class maximise their life chances by being able to understand and communicate effectively in oral, written, and visual language.

While much time is spent teaching reading and writing, children are often expected to "catch" oral language in the course of the day. While this may be acceptable within a busy curriculum for those children from standard English-language backgrounds who have had many opportunities to talk to more able peers and adults, it is clearly discriminatory for the many other children who may enter school with different scores on an oral language measure.

Your job as a teacher of oral language is therefore two-fold. First, to teach children to communicate and, second, to teach children oral language that will help with reading and writing. Table 15 shows these two functions of oral language.

Table 15   Oral Language

COMMUNICATION	AID TO LITERACY
CONVERSATIONS	USING BOOK LANGUAGE
ASKING AND ANSWERING QUESTIONS	USING DECONTEXTUALISED LANGUAGE
DISCUSSION/DEBATE OPINIONS	USING BOOK STRUCTURES
LISTENING	

Communication

Your classroom should be arranged and your program planned so that children have ample opportunity for talk with each other throughout the day. Some teachers of junior classes have found it appropriate to allow children to sit wherever they wish rather than assigning specific seats. This ensures that in the course of the day the children have opportunity to talk to many of their classmates in a variety of different settings.

Be sure that you make time to talk to each child individually and on a personal basis each day. This can often be done before school starts in the morning as children arrive, at an odd moment during the day, or during recess and lunchtime. It is during these conversations that you not only form a close relationship with your children but you are also able to provide a specific oral language model and to monitor ongoing language acquisition.

Ideas to Assist Oral Language Development

Language Experiences

Language Experiences covering the entire curriculum are an excellent medium for oral language development. A description of this approach may be found in Chapter 6. Some topics for Language Experience are listed below.

General Topics

- Use the children's own experiences, such as dreams, first day at school, what do you do in the weekend, etc.
- Photographs of the children engaging in some activities.
- Describe your hand. What does it look like? What does it do?
- Tell imaginary stories, e.g., How I captured the enormous, spiky, fire-breathing, school-eating monster.
- Mystery box, what is inside it, what does it look like?
- Your heart's desire parcel—each child describes what is in it.
- Crystal ball, Magic Telescope—describe what they can see.
- Display an old sweater, boots, etc. Where have they been? Who do they belong to?

Science

- Classroom animals, such as birds, rabbits, mice, etc.
- Snail races.
- Objects that sink/float.
- Blowing bubbles.
- Taste buds to taste salt, sugar, etc.

Cooking

- Pancakes.
- Instant puddings.
- Soup.
- Hokey pokey.
- Mouse traps.
- Chocolate crackles.

Social studies

- Living with handicaps.
- Limited vision.

Art and craft

- Batik.
- Tie-dying.
- Box modelling.

Outside the classroom

- Seasonal walks.
- Describing the weather.
- Watching local workers.
- School trips.
- Unexpected visits, e.g., the fire truck.
- Learning a new skill in physical education, e.g., skipping, balancing.

Morning news

Many teachers include a daily news or show and tell session in their everyday timetable. Sessions such as these provide a perfectly natural environment for teaching young children how to speak clearly and concisely to an audience, to listen actively, and to ask appropriate questions of the speaker. As children become less egocentric you may like to put them into small buzz groups for morning news. As with any group work however, you will need to teach the required group skills before allowing the children to work in this way.

Telling and retelling stories

While many of us place emphasis on reading stories, we often neglect the important oral language tradition of many of our cultures of story telling. Such stories can be factual or fictional, told in the traditional manner adhering to traditional customs, or built up through the medium of drama. The drama example in Chapter 13 could include a specific, daily storytelling segment, where each person in the drama recounts their experiences.

Role-play

Young children learn much about social relationships and the language appropriate to different situations as they play. For children just starting school there is much language to be learned informally from interacting with others in a home corner, a dress-up centre and a shop. Limited only by the imagination of the children, you could set up other areas, e.g., a space station, that would lead to the use of different language.

One class of five- and six-year-olds became people from outer space who had a malfunction in their spaceship and landed in the school playground at night. Because they were fearful, they hid in the classroom. It was here that they talked about and tried to make sense of what they could see. It was here also that they also made decisions about what to do next and talked about the fear that they felt.

Drama

Closely allied to informal role-play is the use of drama as a tool for literacy learning. As well as being a very powerful medium for helping children build concepts and understandings and solve complex problems, it is also a very effective way of extending oral language, particularly for those children whose first language is not English. It involves all children at the level at which they can participate, while the context of the drama provides for much new oral language learning to occur. Reading and writing also occur daily as the children revisit decisions made and revise and rework their ideas.

You can take part in unscripted role-play so that you can facilitate learning both during and after the drama episodes. The drama episodes may take place each day or every other day depending on the time taken over the consolidation and extension activities.

Integrated units of work

When planning your units of work it is a good idea to include learning outcomes and learning experiences that relate directly to oral language. In this way, you will be sure not to leave things to chance. One class of six- and seven-year-olds was working on an integrated unit associated with making and breaking promises. As part of this unit, they studied the story of the Pied Piper. The teacher included the following learning outcomes and learning experiences as part of her planning.

LEARNING OUTCOMES	LEARNING EXPERIENCES
Recount events in a formal manner	Present a daily news bulletin of events.
Interview a person	In pairs one child is reporter, one is the Mayor of Hamelin. Find out what the Mayor intends to do. The same situation was used with one child being the reporter and the other being the Pied Piper.
Express an Opinion	Class discussion on the ethics of the Mayor and the Pied Piper.
Take part in a debate	Children as councillors debate whether or not to pay the Pied Piper.
Describe a scene	Children tell what it looks like inside the mountain.

Listening

In this day and age when children are bombarded with sounds, they often appear to be listening but do not actually hear what is being said. There are many games that foster listening skills, but as with oral language, they seem to have become lost in an overcrowded curriculum. As so much information is available through actively listening, it is important that we take time to teach this skill to young children, bearing in mind that maximum concentration has a limited span.

Oral Language as an Aid to Literacy

Written language is not oral language written down. Although much of the vocabulary may be common to both, each language mode has its own particular conventions. For many young children, the oral language they use to communicate with others is very different from that which is found in the books they are expected to read. Children who have been read to at home enter school already knowing a lot about decontextualised language, book language, and book structure all of which provide important knowledge that assists the acquisition of reading and writing.

Decontextualised language

Conversations between speakers usually revolve around a common theme where each participant is familiar with the context. The more intimate the participants, the less need there is to elaborate. Most of the conversations that take place in families are of this nature, and consequently many children enter school with oral language that is context bound. Children who have been read to frequently have heard many examples of decontextualised language in their bedtime stories, and are able to use such language when the situation arises. For example, after a scuffle in the playground, a child with context-bound language may report the incident to you as "He hit him here, like this, see?" The child able to use decontextualised language may report the incident as "John punched Jason on the neck."

Book language and structure

Decontextualised language is very much the language of books, but book language also encompasses other facets not found in everyday oral language. Book language includes the use of:

Participles:
The little boy watched the **splashing** rain.
Adjectives:
The **friendly** goat ate the toast.
Direct Speech:
"Oh no. We're locked out!"
Sound Effects:
"Wheeeeeee" went the fire truck.
Adverbs:
Slowly and **quietly** the little mouse crept across the floor.
A variety of verbs:
The cat **started** down the path.
Particular nouns:
The **villain** was overcome in the **altercation**.
Different word order:
Up the tree they climbed.

A good way to check if children are becoming able to use book language is to ask a child to tell you about his or her birthday party. You can tell from this how much decontextualised language the child is able to use although the overall interaction should be informal. Next, ask the child to read a story book without words or a picture book that the child cannot yet read independently to a doll or teddy. The child able to use book language should automatically switch to a more formal register.

Monitoring Oral Language Development

Regular informal observations of, and conversations with, the children are the best way to monitor oral language. In this way, you will be able to:

- assess how well they use oral language to communicate;
- note how and if they participate in conversations, ask and answer questions, take part in discussions, express opinions, and follow verbal directions;
- assess how well they are able to use decontextualised and book language;
- note changes in their grammatical structure over time (this will apply particularly to children experiencing difficulty with some aspect of oral language);
- monitor acquisition, especially with children for whom English is not the first language;
- identify children with special ability in language.

From these observations you will be able to:

- group children together for specific teaching (for example, a group of children who are unable to use book language may be drawn together frequently to work at the listening post or to have extra stories read to them);
- choose appropriate grammatical structures when working with particular individuals.

It is important early in the school year to include a formal check of children's oral language along with your other literacy baseline data. To do this you will need to observe children in a variety of formal and informal situations. A checklist to help guide your observations is included in the Appendix.

11 Factual Texts

Accessing, Organising, and Presenting Information

The suggestions given in this chapter can be used with small groups and individuals. Many are also appropriate for whole class instruction. The planning suggestions and classroom activities are all based on current teaching practises and, more importantly, each one has been successfully used in many diverse classrooms.

If you evaluate children's strengths and needs by regular monitoring of their reading, writing, speaking, and listening competencies, you will be able to decide which experiences will assist them in their learning. It is important that every child in your class is included in the evaluation process.

At first, some young readers have difficulty with this genre, so you may consider including narrative texts about factual topics to provide a bridge to more challenging expository genres. Longer non-fiction texts with tables of contents, indexes, chapters, and glossaries can be introduced to beginning readers by being read to them or introduced in a Shared Book approach.

On entry to school, many children are already familiar with narrative writing. They will have heard stories told in this form, and they will often be able to retell an experience or story in their own words. Many will also have had considerable exposure to procedural reading and writing. They may have watched an older person follow a recipe or work out how to use an appliance, for example. Notes, letters, and even diaries could also be part of their preschool experiences. They may have also learned about signs and notices in their community that direct them to places or activities.

Letter writing can be a useful and non-threatening introduction to factual writing for young children. It can provide a writing experience in a meaningful context if it is linked with the composition of "thank you" notes, letters of invitation, requests for information, or letters to friends. A "Post Box" set up in the classroom with paper, envelopes, and used postage stamps for the children to write notes to each other will be a real incentive for them to pick up their pencils and start writing.

Diary writing can extend children's writing to a range of genres, such as recounts, descriptions, and reports. Conferencing with you, a peer, or an older child may expand the recount, description, or report through questioning, such as "That sounds interesting, tell me more about it," or "I'm not quite sure what you mean here. How else could we say that?"

Exploring a range of factual writing in the classroom provides experiences that can then be linked with the styles of writing children will find in book collections and other factual texts.

Being introduced to factual texts right from the start of their time at school provides children with real learning experiences that link their classroom activities with their everyday lives outside school. They learn to read texts to gain information and to distinguish between fact and fiction. Through exposure to a wide variety of genres, the children begin to recognise how different types of text are organised. They also begin to identify the language features that are common to both fiction and non-fiction, as well as those that are particular to each of the separate genres.

When making suggestions for the use of factual texts, we have made the assumption that you will be selecting texts to suit the needs and abilities of the children and that you will be planning reading/language learning outcomes as well as content area outcomes.

As Professor Marie Clay says, "Reading is a meaning-making, problem-solving activity" and the process skills of social studies and science are closely related to reading comprehension skills. Reading and writing can easily be integrated with other curriculum areas in your classroom.

Types of Factual Text

TYPE OF TEXT	PURPOSE
Procedural or instructional	To follow directions, e.g., "how to" texts.
Expository	To explain and to supply knowledge.
Narrative	To evoke a personal response.

12 Technology and Literacy

Most children come to school already knowing a great deal about technology. They are familiar with technological advances in the preparation and storing of food, sending and receiving messages, and transport. Most families have cars, stoves, television sets, telephones, and many also have computers, video recorders, and microwave ovens.

Technologically, your responsibility as a teacher is twofold. Firstly, you can help children learn more about technology and how it has impacted on the environment and the economy, and influenced the lives of peoples in different times and in different places. Secondly, you can assist children use technology and the processes involved in technology to help them learn.

Although technology is often linked in the curriculum with science, it is a cross-curricular subject that has applications in mathematics, music, health, physical education, social studies, art, and literature.

Central to the learning processes in technology learning is the design process. A chart showing the stages involved in the design process appears below.

Table 16   Stages of Design

Identify the need/problem.

Prepare the design brief.

Think about the problem.

Research the problem.

Develop ideas.

Plan and design a model.

Make the model.

Test and evaluate.

For young children already familiar with the many delightful stories in literature, integrating literature and technology is a logical starting place. The following example shows how *Mr Gumpy's Outing* (John Burningham, Jonathan Cape) is used with a technological theme.

The problem or need which has been identified in the story is where you start and this may affect everyone or only one person. After reading *Mr Gumpy's Outing* to the class, the children can discuss at the class level or in small groups, the problems and needs faced by Mr Gumpy and his friends. They can then offer some possible solutions.

Some examples may be:

"Mr Gumpy needs to get a bigger boat."
"Mr Gumpy needs a boat where different people and different animals can sit in different places."
"Mr Gumpy needs a boat that won't tip over."
"They need something to help those who can't swim to get out of the river."
"The problem is that the animals don't do what

93

they are told."

"The problem is that the children and animals get bored and start being naughty."

If children can only identify problems, you can generate further discussion to ask them to identify needs that would help solve the problem.

For example:

> Make a BoT that is Big enuf for anamls and Peepl

> Make a boat that will not tip over

> Make a boat that has difrent roogs for difrent animals

Thinking about the problem

This activity can be done in many ways but one of the most popular is to brainstorm. Very young children and those for whom this type of learning is new will probably work better in a whole class grouping with your support to start with. In this way, you can act as the scribe for their ideas. Others may prefer to work in co-operative groups while some children will prefer to work with a close friend or alone. At this stage, it is important to encourage creativity and originality in thinking and accept all responses as valid and important. The following general questions may offer a guide to thinking:

"How much time have I got to solve the problem?"
"What materials are available to me?"
"How big must it be?"
"What shape will it be?"
"What will it look like?"
"Can I make it work?"
"Will it be safe?"
"Can I construct it?"
"Will it be useful to other people?"

A web for Mr Gumpy's boat may look like this:

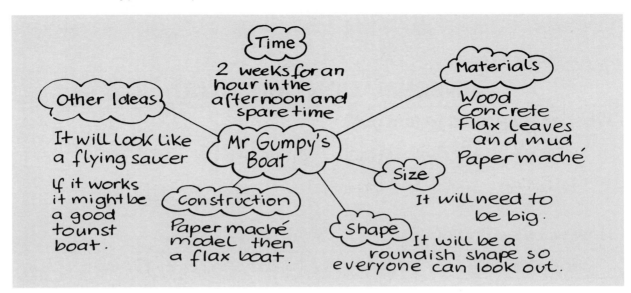

Researching the problem

This is the part of the design process that requires children to use information and information technology skills. Having already recorded what they already know about the topic, the children now need to pose the following questions:

"What do I need to find out?"
"Where will I go to find out?"

"What skills do I need to extract the relevant information?"
"How will I organise my information so that it is useful for my purpose?"

A sample checklist for Mr Gumpy appears below. A blank of this checklist is available for copying in the Appendix.

INFORMATION CHECKLIST

What do I/we need to find out?

What flotes and sinks
How to bild a boat

How will I/we find out?	✓	Boatyard
Visit in community	✓	Ask Jesses Dad
Ask people	✓	Look cop boat books
Visit library		
Use video		
Use database	✓	To find boat books
Experiment	✓	Sinking and floating
Which skills do I/we need?		
Questioning	✓	Writ kweschuns to ask
Listening	✓	Lissen to cmsers
Use Dewey system	✓	Look up boat books
Use database	✓	Look up boat books
Use reference material	✓	
Use table of contents	✓	
Use index	✓	
Use sub-headings	✓	
Use diagrams/pictures	✓	
Skim/scan/keywords	✓	
Use camera	✓	Take pictns of boats
Use tape recorder	✓	cot boatyard
Use video		
Use computer	✓	
Make notes	✓	
Make charts	✓	

Developing ideas

Armed with all this information, it is now time for the children to start developing ideas that will ultimately lead to making a decision about which is the best of all their ideas. This may be the same as their original idea, a new version of the original idea, or a completely new idea.

At this point, children should be encouraged to make rough notes and sketches to help them clarify their thinking. Once again you can act as scribe for very young children if necessary. You would expect lots of discussion at all stages of the design process, especially now as children talk to each other to see if what they have planned both solves the problem as stated in the design brief, and is practical and workable.

Simon and Jesse have decided to make a boat that has separate compartments for each of the animals to help stop them squabbling. They want each of the animals to be able to look out so that they won't get bored.

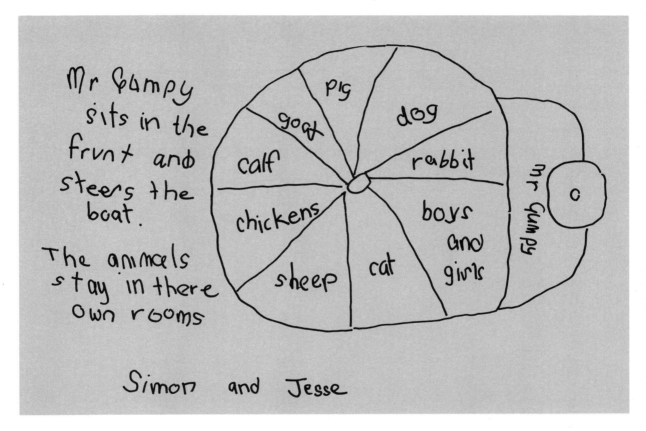

Mr Gumpy sits in the frunt and steers the boat.

The animals stay in there own rooms

pig
goat
dog
calf
rabbit
chickens
boys and girls
Mr Gumpy
0
sheep
cat

Simon and Jesse

Planning and designing

Planning involves making a careful drawing of the solution. These drawings should include all measurements, the material(s) it is to be made of, and how it is made, including special details and features.

Much discussion has taken place between Simon and Jesse and other children working on similar projects, before Simon and Jesse decided that a rectangular boat would be easier for them to construct. They also made modifications to the placement of the compartments, using smaller compartments for smaller animals, and trying to keep those that would chase each other apart.

They decided to use a soap powder box as a frame to build their papier mâché onto, and to attach a smaller box onto the front for Mr Gumpy to sit in to steer the boat. They have decided to make the model of the boat while they are researching ways to make it move through the water.

Their plan is not drawn to scale but their measurements of the soap powder box are accurate. They have used the computer to label their plan and write the instructions for both the plan and the model making.

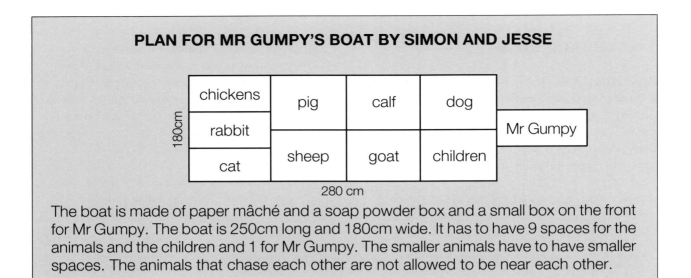

PLAN FOR MR GUMPY'S BOAT BY SIMON AND JESSE

The boat is made of paper mâché and a soap powder box and a small box on the front for Mr Gumpy. The boat is 250cm long and 180cm wide. It has to have 9 spaces for the animals and the children and 1 for Mr Gumpy. The smaller animals have to have smaller spaces. The animals that chase each other are not allowed to be near each other.

The design should tell the child, or anyone else who may be going to make the model, how to go about it. It should state such instructions as whether any new skills are needed, what is to be made first, and how accurate the measurements need to be.

INSTRUCTIONS FOR MAKING THE MODEL OF MR GUMPY'S BOAT BY SIMON AND JESSE

You will need:

A soap powder box.
A small box.
Newspaper cut into strips.
Wallpaper paste or glue.
Tissue paper.
Paint.

What to do:

Cut one of the big sides out of the soap powder box.
Cut one of the big sides out of the small box.
Staple the small box onto the front of the big box.
Dip the strips of newspaper in the glue and then stick them on the boxes.
Cover both the boxes and wrap some strips round the small box so it won't fall off.
Wait for it to dry.
Put on some more paper.
When it is dry cover it with tissue paper.
When it is dry paint the boat.

Realising

Realising is turning the planning and designing that the children did on paper, into reality.

Testing and evaluating

Did the design solve the problem? Does it need some small alterations? Does it not solve the problem at all?

By going back to the original problem or need and the design brief, the children can ascertain how well they did as inventors. If part of the process has broken down, there will be a need to revisit that area and take a fresh look.

Simon and Jesse solved part of the problem, i.e., how to separate the animals. They then returned to the beginning of the design process again to see if they could decide the best way to power the boat so that Mr Gumpy would have more time with his friends.

The evaluation sheet below is designed to be used by you and the child in collaboration. It can also be used for self evaluation by the child or as a teacher's evaluation tool. It should help both you and the children determine how well they are able to use technological processes. Charts that are useful in helping children organise their planning are also available for copying in the Appendix.

TECHNOLOGY PROCESS EVALUATION SHEET

Name Simon   **Date** 21/9/93

Did I :	Fully	Partially	Need more help
Understand the problem/need?	✓		
Think creatively?		✓	
Talk with others about my ideas?		✓	
Collect relevant information?			✓
Use appropriate research skills?			✓
Record my results?		✓	
Develop my ideas?		✓	
Plan and sketch?	✓		
Use appropriate materials and tools?	✓		
Modify where necessary?		✓	
Share my findings?	✓		
Know what to do if things went wrong?			✓

Comments:
Simon's strengths lie in his ability to understand problems - plan and sketch solutions and share final results. He tends to rely on others for ideas and is not keen to record results in detail. He needs more help with researching relevant information and getting back on track after a difficulty.

Learning Experiences and Outcomes

It is important that you have clearly defined language outcomes in mind in addition to your technology and other curriculum area objectives.

Some technology learning experiences and outcomes you could consider are:

Learning Experiences	Learning Outcomes
Brainstorm ideas of Mr Gumpy's problem. Record as a web.	Use imagination to explore and produce ideas.
Choose the appropriate material to construct a model of a boat.	Explore and use a variety of materials to design and construct things.
Sort materials into those which float and those which sink.	Recognise that materials have different properties which make them more suitable for use in different situations.
Choose materials and tools available in the classroom to make a boat.	Make choices between available materials.
Use the appropriate tools to make a boat.	Join materials in basic ways.
State the rules for using equipment such as saws, hammers, glues, etc.	Use equipment safely.
Write a design brief, draw sketches, draw plans, write labels, and write instructions.	Reproduce and develop ideas by drawing, working with materials and equipment, model making, and writing.
Make a model of a boat.	Make models of simple structures.
Compare finished work with design brief.	Evaluate finished work against original purpose.
Share ideas with friends, evaluate performance with the teacher.	Talk about the process of design and construction.

An overall teacher's initial plan for Mr Gumpy's Outing using a cross curricular approach focusing on literacy and technology, may look like this:

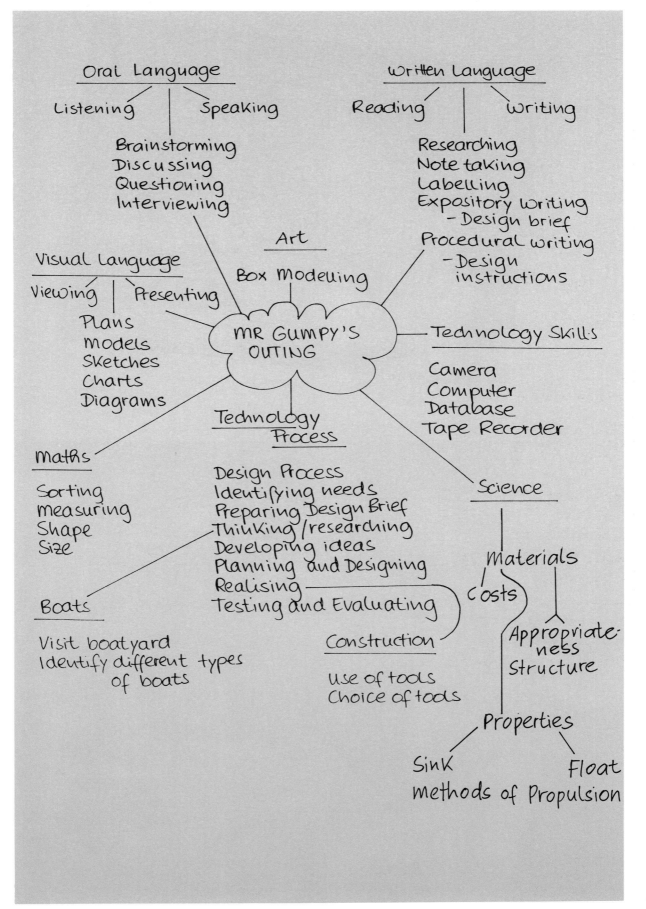

Oral Language
Listening | Speaking

Brainstorming
Discussing
Questioning
Interviewing

Written Language
Reading | Writing

Researching
Note taking
Labelling
Expository Writing
— Design brief
Procedural writing
— Design
   instructions

Art
Box Modelling

Visual Language
Viewing | Presenting

Plans
Models
Sketches
Charts
Diagrams

MR GUMPY'S OUTING

Technology Skills

Camera
Computer
Database
Tape Recorder

Maths

Sorting
Measuring
Shape
Size

Technology
Process

Design Process
Identifying needs
Preparing Design Brief
Thinking/researching
Developing ideas
Planning and Designing
Realising
Testing and Evaluating

Science

Materials
Costs
Appropriate-
   ness
Structure

Boats

Visit boatyard
Identify different types
   of boats

Construction

Use of tools
Choice of tools

Properties

Sink   Float
Methods of Propulsion

13 Drama as a Medium for Learning

The following example of an unscripted drama uses the story *Pollution* (Sandra Iversen, Wonder World II) as motivation.

Steps for Using Drama

1 Read the story to the children.
2 Rewrite the text in large print as a wall story. Encourage the children to illustrate this wall story. Enlarging the story and keeping it on the wall ensures that every child has regular access to the original story as the drama unfolds.
3 If necessary, alter your classroom environment to make sure you have enough space for the children to move around freely.
4 Make a card label (about 20 x 5 centimetres in size) for each child to wear around their neck. The roles they choose for themselves are written on the labels.
5 Explain the drama to the children.

"We are going to be people living in a little village not too far away from a big chemical factory. When we are the people in the drama, we will wear labels around our necks. When we take these off, we will be the children in this classroom again."

6 Give each child a label. Move to the space.

"When you have decided which person in the village you want to be, I want you to start going about your daily work."

7 Decide on your own role.

Choose a role that the villagers will see as having some authority, or choose to be someone who lives on the outskirts of the village nearer the factory, e.g., a farmer. Bring back the news that there has been an explosion at the chemical factory, that toxic fumes are drifting towards the village, and that the river the village depends on for water has been polluted. Call a meeting of the villagers to decide what to do.

8 From this point on, be guided by what the children say.

Each class of children will come up with different solutions to the problem that has been posed. However, when the children leave the drama each day, you can help them clarify and extend their thinking. Make sure that after each drama the children remove the labels and leave the feelings and emotions that the drama evokes in the drama situation.

The following example comes from a class of six-year-old children.

Episode 1

In the drama
As the village people go about their work, a farmer (the teacher) comes to tell them what he or she has seen. The farmer takes the villagers to see the disaster. Everyone goes back to the village and talks about what they have seen and what they should do.

Out of the drama
The children made a "Possibilities and Outcomes" chart and drew pictures of themselves as villagers. They also co-operatively wrote a diary of the day's events. This was built up daily into a wall story timeline.

Episode 2

In the drama
The villagers go back with the farmer to see the fume cloud approaching. They then go down to the river to see what is happening to it. They tell each other what they see and how they feel. They return to the village and continue their discussion.

Out of the drama

The children:

- Revised the ideas on the possibilities chart in light of the day's events;
- Categorised possible solutions to get the main ideas;

- Made a tally chart to reflect which ideas they thought were the best;
- Painted what they saw and wrote captions for their paintings;
- Wrote poems expressing how they felt;
- Wrote the diary of the day's events.

Episode 3

In the drama

The villagers discuss the main things they decided to do to avert disaster, e.g., dam the river and build underground bunkers.

They discuss:

- How they will do it;
- Where they will get the materials;
- How long it will take;
- How many helpers will be needed;
- Will everyone help or would some people be better doing other things, e.g., cooking meals for the workers?

Out of the drama

On separate charts, the children recorded the results of the discussion. They continued to write the diary of the day's events.

Episode 4

In the drama

The villagers, reminded that time is running short, decide that the solutions they have chosen cannot be realised in the time available. They decide to evacuate the village and discuss what they will take with them.

Out of the drama

The children:

- Individually drew up lists of important things to take;
- Described why these things were important to them;

- Transferred this information onto a chart;
- Wrote their diary of the day's events.

Episode 5

In the drama

The villagers collect their important belongings and start to evacuate. They express their feelings at leaving. They are all to be taken by air to a faraway place where they will be resettled. They take a last look at their homes from the sky above.

Out of the drama

The children painted and wrote about what they saw from the air and how they felt. The diary of the day's events was written up.

Episode 6

In the drama

A year has gone by and the villagers are now settled into a new village. Everyone has had to make some changes in their lives and some have changed jobs. They meet to discuss old times and to talk over the decisions they made.

A TV reporter (the teacher) arrives to tell them of another bad case of pollution where a village is being threatened. The reporter wants the villagers to tell the media how they went about making the decisions they made and what their advice to the people now threatened would be.

The TV reporter tapes these responses as the villagers form their evaluation of events and apply the knowledge they have learned.

You can use these responses to evaluate how well the children are able to apply the knowledge they gained during the drama.

Glossary

Ability Grouping
The grouping of children with similar needs for instructional purposes. These groups should be constantly adjusted, in response to the changing needs of the children.

Balanced Language Program
A quality literacy program that encompasses the best approaches for oral, written, and visual language.

Brainstorming
A strategy for developing creative thought and surfacing prior knowledge. Ideas are presented but not evaluated until all possible suggestions have been made. Brainstorming can assist you in finding out children's prior knowledge of a topic. The teacher usually records the children's ideas in chart form so that the class can refer to them and revise them later.

Cinquain
A five-line poem in the following format:

Line 1	one word	title
Line 2	two words	describes the title
Line 3	three words	expresses movement
Line 4	four words	expresses feeling
Line 5	one word	synonym for the title

Comprehension
The interpretation of the print on the page into a meaningful message. This will depend on the readers prior knowledge, cultural and social background, and their ongoing comprehension monitoring strategies.

Concepts about Print
These include book handling skills, looking at print, directionality, sequencing and locating skills, punctuation, and concepts of letters and words.

Cues
Readers integrate several sources of information, or cues, to monitor ongoing reading comprehension.

Decontextualised Language
Oral language that is not dependent on the participants being present at the event or the surrounding context for interpretation.

Graphic Organisers
Graphic organisers make a visual relationship between ideas. The function of an organiser is to provide a scaffold for new ideas by activating relevant prior knowledge. They can emphasise both similarities and differences, e.g., Venn diagrams.

Guided Reading
Students work in ability groups to read as independently as possible a text that you have selected for them and introduced to them. This text will be at the group's instructional level, that is, the students will be able to read it with 90%-94% accuracy.

Guided Writing
A small group of students work with you to write a story, an item of news, a retelling of a familiar story, or a recount of an experience. It may also involve you working individually with a student to scaffold the task of writing words and sentences.

Independent Reading
Students engage in independent reading (95%-100% accuracy) daily in order to build reading mileage, build fluency, and practice integrating cues and orchestrating strategies.

Innovation
The creation of a new story based on a familiar pattern or theme. Innovation may include renaming characters, adding episodes, changing endings, making a new story using the same story structure, or making a new version of the same story.

Justified Print
The positioning of print on the page so that each line ends either a sentence or a phrase.

Language Experience
A process that leads children to the understanding that what they think about they can talk about, what they talk about they can write about, and what they write about, they themselves and others can read. Because the children have been involved in the experience and created the story in their own language, this provides the semantic, syntactic, and graphophonic prior knowledge that scaffolds the reading task.

Listening Post
Sets of headphones attached to a single tape player. Children listen to audiotapes of books while reading the book.

Mapping chart
A method of recording using lines to map from one object to another to show a relationship.

Monitoring reading
Students use a variety of strategies to monitor reading. These include strategies that (a) maintain fluency, such as bringing oral language, prior knowledge of the world, the story and the print to make tentative predictions; (b) enable students to monitor and check, such as searching, checking, and self-correcting; and (c) that help problem-solve new words, such as making links from known to unknown words, using context and oral language expectations, breaking words into parts, and using analogies and letter sound knowledge.

Phonological Cues
Readers use their knowledge of letter/sound and sound/letter relationships to predict and confirm reading.

Possibilities/Outcomes Chart
A chart showing possible solutions to a problem on one side and the resultant outcomes on the other.

Reading levels
Independent: 95%-100% accuracy
Instructional: 90%-94% accuracy
Frustrational: 89% or less accuracy
These scores should be interpreted in conjunction with comprehension from retelling.

Reading to Children
A scheduled time each day in which you read a story or book to the class.

Record of Reading Behaviour
A neutral observation during which you record, using a standard set of symbols, everything the child says as s/he reads a book you have chosen.

Recount
A story written in the first person recounting an event or series of events.

Retelling
Retelling can be written or oral. Children are expected to retell as much of a story as they can remember. Retelling includes everything in the story, in contrast to a summary, which is brief and has only one relevant main idea.

Scaffolding
Scaffolding is used to describe the support that enables a learner to complete a task or achieve a goal that would have been unattainable without assistance. As the learner becomes more proficient, the scaffold is withdrawn. Ultimately the child is able to perform the task independently and internalises the behaviour. For example, in Shared Reading you scaffold the task by reading the story to the children first, thus taking the initial responsibility for all the decoding and some of the meaning making.

Semantic cues
Readers use their prior knowledge, sense of the story, and pictures to assist with prediction and confirmation of the meaning of text.

Semantic Web
Beginning with a central idea, a semantic web is used to extend knowledge and ideas in graphic form. A web may be used before a topic to surface and extend and clarify prior knowledge, and after a topic to include and check new learning.

Sociogram
A diagram connecting characters in a story and showing the relationship between them.

Syntactic cues
Readers use their oral language and prior knowledge of how language works, e.g., word order, to assist with prediction and confirmation of text.

Tally chart
A chart, usually counted in groups of five, used to show quantity, e.g., ////

Task Management Board
A board listing set and optional activities for children to engage in. Children can then work independently by consulting the board, which leaves the teacher free to work with individuals or groups. You change the board daily.

Timeline
A chart showing information in chronological order.

Unscripted role-play
A drama or role-play where there is no prewritten script. The children respond to a problem that needs to be resolved from the point of view of the roles they take.

Venn Diagram
A diagram consisting of two or three intersecting circles to visually represent similarities and differences between texts, characters, etc.

Visual cues
Readers use their knowledge of graphemes to predict and confirm text. This can be at the word, syllable, or letter level, the most powerful being the largest chunk of visual information.

References

If you would like to read further on the ideas expressed in this book, may we suggest that you consult the following:

ADAMS, M. J. *Beginning to Read. Thinking and Learning About Print.* MIT Press, 1990.

ADAMS, M. J. "Why Not Phonics and Whole Language?" in *All Language and the Creation of Literacy* [W. Willis (ed)]. Orton Dyslexia Society, 1991.

ALLINGTON, R. L. "Fluency: The Neglected Goal" in *Reading Teacher,* 36:6, 1983.

BROWN, H. and MATHIE, V. *Inside Whole Language. A Classroom View.* PETA, 1990.

BRUNER J. "Vygotsky: A Historical and Conceptual Perspective" in *Culture Communication and Cognition. Vygotskian Perspectives* [J. Wertsch (ed)]. Cambridge University Press, 1986.

CAMBOURNE, B. *The Whole Story.* Ashton Scholastic, 1988.

CAZDEN, C. B. "Adults' Assistance to Language Development: Scaffolds, Models and Direct Instruction" in *Developing Literacy* [C. B. Cazden (ed)]. IRA, 1983.

CAZDEN, C. B. *Interactions Between Maori Children and Pakeha Teachers.* Auckland Reading Association, 1988.

CLAY, M. M. "Introducing A New Storybook to Young Readers" in *Reading Teacher,* 45:4, 1991.

CLAY, M. M. *An Observation Survey of Early Literacy Achievement.* Heinemann, 1993.

CLAY, M. M. *What Did I Write?* Heinemann Education, 1975.

CLAY, M. M. *Becoming Literate. The Construction of Inner Control.* Heinemann Education, 1993.

CLAY, M. M. "Engaging With the School System. A Study of Interaction in New Entrant Classrooms" in *N.Z. Journal of Educational Studies,* 20:1, 1983.

CULLINAN, B. E. *Children's Literature in the Reading Programme.* IRA, 1987.

CULLINAN, B. E. *More Children's Literature in the Reading Programme.* IRA, 1992.

CZERNIEWSKA, P. *Learning About Writing.* Blackwell Publishers, 1992.

DEPREE, H. F. *Children's Early Writing.* An unpublished paper, 1979.

DEPREE, H. and IVERSEN, S. *Wonder World. A Balanced Language Programme.* Lands End Publishing, 1992.

DEPREE, H. and IVERSEN, S. *Wonder World II. The Real World Around Us.* Lands End Publishing, 1993.

DOWNING, J. *Reading and Reasoning.* W & R Chambers, 1979.

ELLEY, W. "What Do Children Learn From Being Read To?", *SET 1,* NZCER, 1985.

GOSWAMI, U. and BRYANT, P. *Phonological Skills and Learning to Read.* Erlbaum and Associates, 1990.

HOYTE, L. "Many Ways of Knowing: Using Drama, Oral Interactions and the Visual Arts to Enhance Reading Comprehension" in *Reading Teacher* , 45:8, 1992.

IDLE, I.K. *Hands-On Technology.* Stanley Thomas Ltd., 1991.

LIBERMAN, I. Y. and LIBERMAN, A. M. "Whole Language v Code Emphasis: Underlying Assumptions and Their Implications for Reading Instruction" in *Annals of Dyslexia*, 40, 1990.

MOLL, L. C. *Vygotsky and Education. Instructional Implications and Applications of Sociohistorical Psychology.* Cambridge University Press, 1990.

OLSON, M. W. and GEE, T. C. "Content Reading Instruction in the Primary Grades: Perceptions and Strategies" in *Reading Teacher*, 45:4, 1991.

PETERS, M. L. "Teacher Variables in Spelling" in *Spelling: Task and Learner* [Wade and Wedell (eds)]. University of Birmingham Press, 1974.

SMITH, F. "Reading Like a Writer" in *Language Arts*, 60:5, 1983.

STANOVICH, K. E. "Romance and Reality" in *Reading Teacher*, 47:4, 1994.

STRICKLAND, D. and MORROW, L. *Emerging Literacy.* IRA, 1990.

THOMPSON, G. B., TUNMER, W. E. and NICHOLSON, T. *Reading Acquisition Processes.* Multilingual Matters, 1993.

TICKLE, L. *Design and Technology in Primary School Classrooms.* P.A. Falmer Press, 1990.

TRELEASE, J. *The New Read Aloud Handbook.* Penguin, 1989.

TUNMER, W. E. and CHAPMAN, J. W. "To Guess Or Not to Guess: That is the Question: Metacognitive Stategy Training, Phonological Recoding Skill and Beginning Reading" in *Reading Forum.* NZRA, 1993.

WILSON, J. "Concept Mapping: What Have You Got In Mind?" in *Reading Around*, Series 4. Australian Reading Association, 1991.

WOOD, D., BRUNER, J. S. and ROSS, G. "The Role of Tutoring in Problem Solving" in *Child Psychiatry*, 17, 1976.

EARLY READING BEHAVIOURS CHECKLIST

Name .... **Age** .... **Date** ....

Behaviour	Always	Sometimes	Never
Handles books appropriately			
Identifies cover, author, etc.			
Demonstrates direction & return sweep			
Matches one-to-one			
Recognises some known words in isolation			
Reruns in order to search and check			
At unknown word searches using:			
picture cues			
story meaning cues			
language structure cues			
word cues			
letter and letter cluster knowledge			
analogies			
After miscue checks on reading using:			
picture cues			
story meaning cues			
language structure cues			
word cues			
letter and letter cluster knowledge			
analogies			
Self corrects			
Reads fluently/phrases appropriately			

Early Reading Checkpoint

Class ....

Teacher ....

Date ....

														Names
														Behaviour
														Handles books appropriately
														Identifies cover, author
														Demonstrates direction
														Matches one-to-one
														Recognises known words
														Reruns
														At unknown word searches using:
														picture cues
														story meaning cues
														language structure cues
														word cues
														letter and cluster cues
														analogies
														After miscue checks using:
														picture cues
														story meaning cues
														language structure cues
														word cues
														letter and cluster cues
														analogies
														self corrects
														reads fluently/phrases appropriately

RECORD OF READING BEHAVIOUR

Name:		Title:	
Age:		Series:	Seen
Date: / /		Stage:	Unseen

Calculations

Error Rate $\frac{RW}{E}$ = 1:

Accuracy %

S/C Rate $\frac{(E + SC)}{SC}$ = 1:

Level: Easy   Instr   Hard

Understanding from Retelling/Questioning

Characters	Yes	....	No
Setting	Yes	....	No
Plot	Yes	....	No
Inferences	Yes	....	No

Competencies (circle predominant behaviours)

1 on 1 matching   Directionality   Fluent Reading

At an unknown word

Makes no attempt   Seeks help   Reruns   Reads on

Attempts using   Letter/sound knowledge   Meaning   Syntax

After an error

Ignores   Seeks help   Reruns   Attempts s/c

Self-corrects using   Letter/sound knowledge   Meaning   Syntax

	E	SC	E msv	SC msv

Record of Reading Behaviour (continued)

			Cues used	
	E	SC	E	SC
TOTAL				

EARLY WRITING BEHAVIOURS CHECKLIST

Name .... **Age** .... **Date** ....

Behaviour	Always	Sometimes	Never
Forms alphabet letters			
Has direction/return sweep			
Leaves space between words			
Uses initial consonants			
Uses dominant consonants			
Has consonant framework			
Uses some vowels			
Makes close approximations			
Writes some words independently			
Locates unknown words in environment			
Uses upper/lower case letters			
Uses punctuation			
Writes one sentence			
Writes two sentences			
Writes a page			
Generates quality ideas			
Sustains ideas over a story			
Writes in different genres			
Proof reads			
Edits			

ANALYSIS OF STORY WRITING

Name .... Date ....

Meaning

Structure

Story structure/length

Language structure

Spelling

Punctuation

Handwriting

Extra information

Strategies for teaching

FIRST YEAR FORMAL CHECK

Name .... Age .... Date ....

WRITING

Check the statements that apply:

Child is unable to trace first name

Child is able to trace first name

Child is almost able to write first name

Child is able to write both names

Child can write some words independently

Words written independently are:

Child can write a story

Story analysis:

Number of sentences

Number of identifiable approximated spellings

Number of words written correctly

Appropriate use of upper/lower case letters

Punctuation

Comment on any other signficant factors in written language:

ORAL LANGUAGE

Name .... Age .... Date ....

Check and date the statements that apply:

English is not the child's first language _____

The first language is _____

Speaks confidently in the first language _____

Speaks confidently in English _____

Speaks confidently in a classroom situation _____

Speaks confidently to an audience _____

Can ask and answer questions _____

Speaks only with friends in informal situations _____

Mostly uses one word statements _____

Speaks in simple sentences _____

Can use complex language structures _____

Often uses structures that are different from standard English _____

Can use decontextualized language _____

Can use book language and structures _____

Can follow one direction _____

Can follow a sequence of three or more directions _____

Comment on any other significant factors of oral language:

READING			WRITING	ORAL LANGUAGE
TEXT	**Strengths**	**Weaknesses**		
WORDS	**Strengths**	**Weaknesses**		
LETTERS	**Strengths**	**Weaknesses**		

WHAT I KNOW

What I know about	What I have learned about ....
What can I do with this information?	

INFORMATION CHECKLIST

What do I/we need to find out?

How will I/we find out?		
Visit in community		
Ask people		
Visit library		
Use video		
Use database		
Experiment		
Which skills do I/we need?		
Questioning		
Listening		
Use Dewey system		
Use database		
Use reference material		
Use table of contents		
Use index		
Use sub-headings		
Use diagrams/pictures		
Skim/scan/keywords		
Use camera		
Use tape recorder		
Use video		
Use computer		
Make notes		
Make charts		

Name .... **Research Topic** **Date** ....

I want to know:

My hypothesis is:

I will look for information in:

My research found out:

PROBLEMS

SOLUTIONS

Story Chart for ....

Written by ....

Where the story takes place:

Characters in the story:

What happened:

The problem:

The solution:

What the story is really about:

Values brought out in the story:

Descriptive language used:

STORY OUTLINE FOR ....

Author:

Publisher:

Date:

Setting/Main Characters:

The Problem:

Sequence of the story:

The solution to the problem:

Story Theme:
What the story is about:

The point of the story:

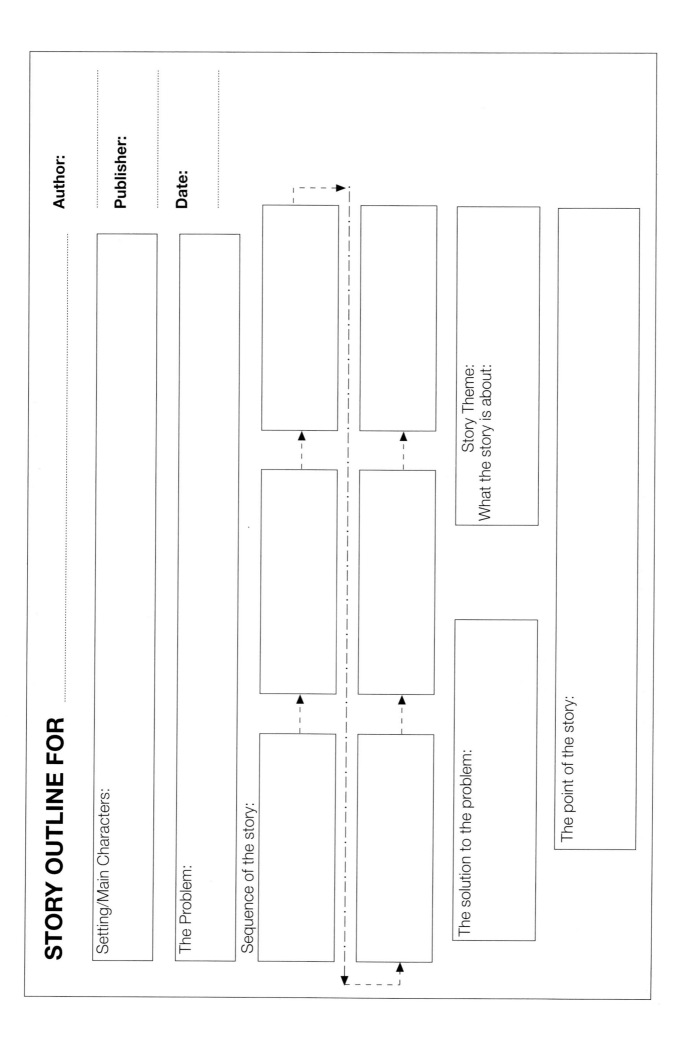

Venn Diagram to Compare and Contrast the Stories

.... and ....

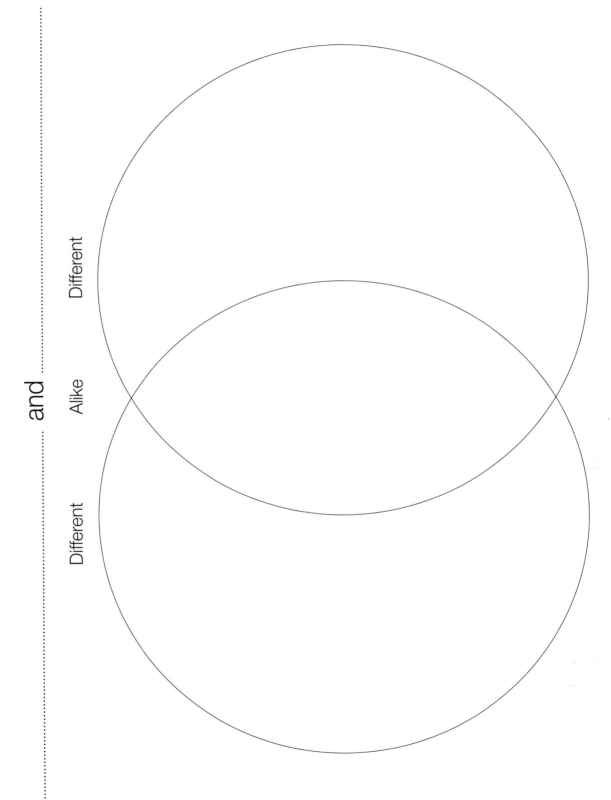

Different

Alike

Different

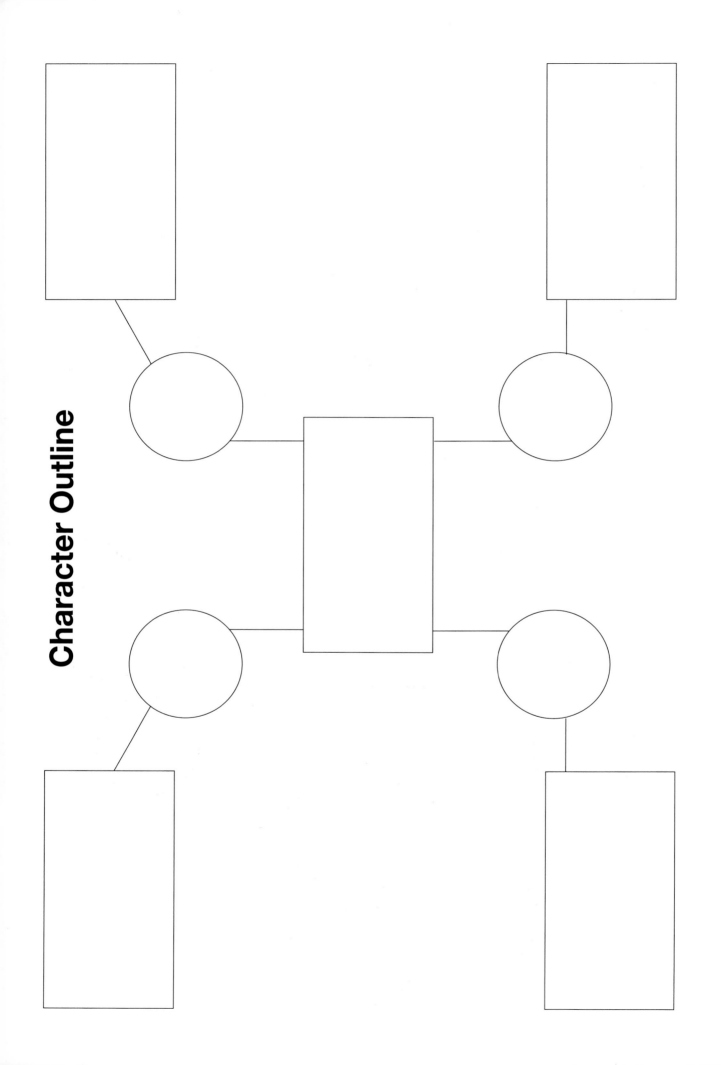

Character Outline

Character outline

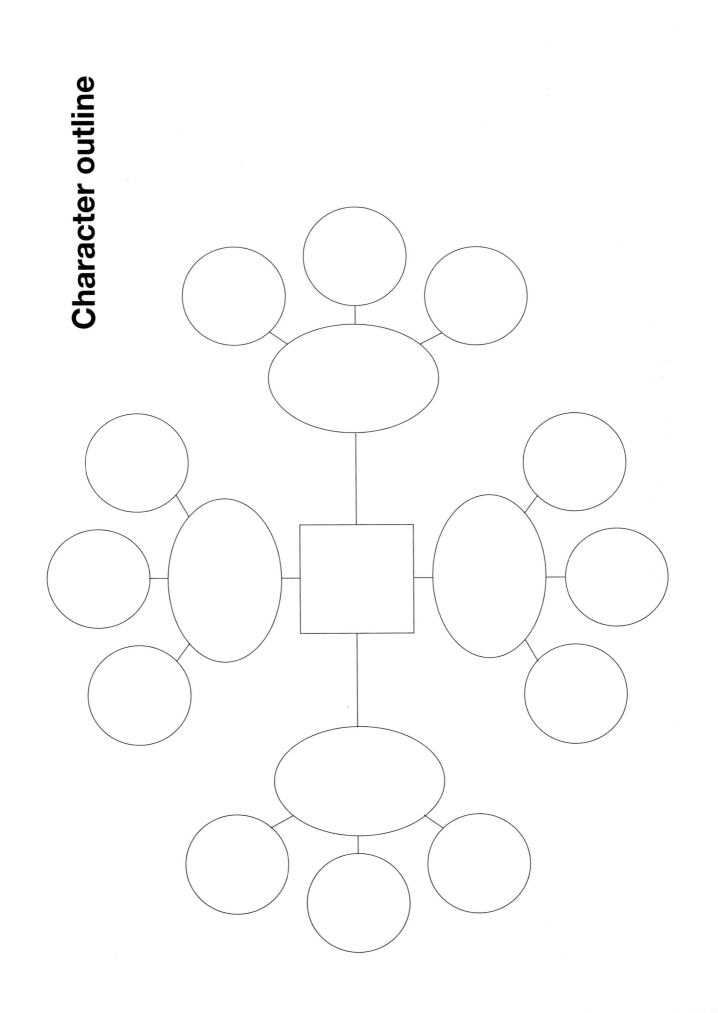

Error rate / Accuracy percentage Table

This table has been devised to assist you with the quick conversion from error rate to percentage accuracy using the following formula.

$$\text{Accuracy \%} = \left\{ 100 - \frac{E}{RW} \right\} \times 100$$

Error Rate	Accuracy%	Reading Level	Reading Approach
1:200	99.5		
1:100	99	Easy,	
1:50	98	Independent	Independent
1:35	97	Reading	Reading
1:25	96	Level	
1:20	95		
1:17	94		
1:14	93	Instructional	Guided
1:12.5	92	Reading	Reading
1:11.75	91	Level	
1:10	90		
1:9	89		
1:8	87.5	Hard,	Shared Reading
1:7	85.5	Frustrational	
1:6	83	Reading	
1:5	80	Level	
1:4	75		
1:3	66		Reading to Children
1:2	50		